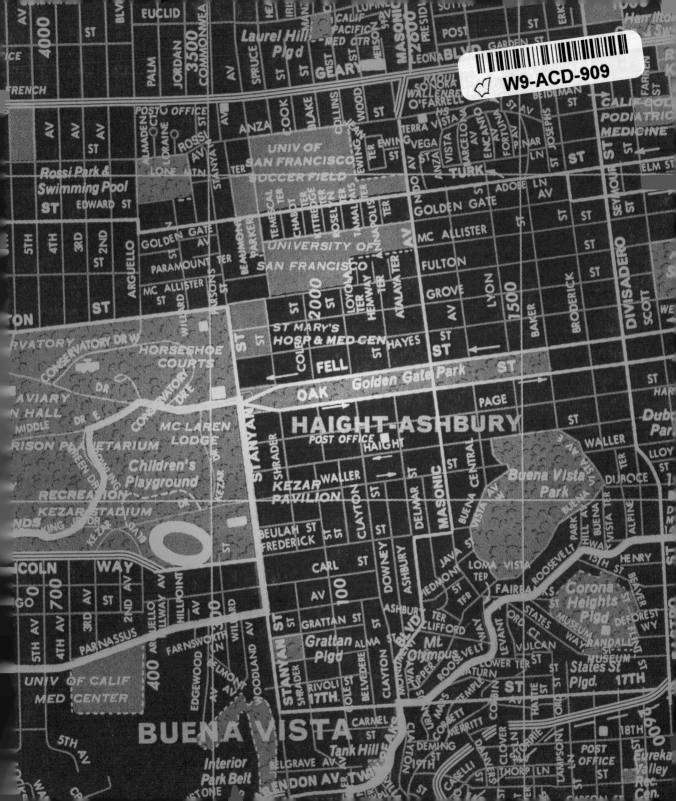

BENEATH THE
DIAMOND
SKY

HAIGHT-ASHBURY 1965–1970

BARNEY HOSKYNS

SIMON &
SCHUSTER
EDITIONS

Then take me disappearin' through the smoke rings of my mind,
Down the foggy ruins of time, far past the frozen leaves,
The haunted, frightened trees, out to the windy beach,
Far from the twisted reach of crazy sorrow.

YES

TO DANCE BENEATH THE DIAMOND SKY
with one hand waving free,

Silhouetted by the sea, circled by the circus sands,
With all memory and fate driven beneath the waves,
Let me forget about today until tomorrow.

Lyric: Bob Dylan, "Mr. Tambourine Man"

BENEATH THE
DIAMOND
SKY

SIMON & SCHUSTER EDITIONS

Rockefeller Center
1230 Avenue of the Americas
New York, NY 10020

SIMON & SCHUSTER EDITIONS and colophon are trademarks
of Simon & Schuster Inc.

Design and art direction by Simon Jennings.
Text image generation by Amanda Allchin, London.
Studio photography by Ben Jennings, London.
Litho reproduction by Radstock Repro, Bath.
Printed by Artegraphica, Verona, Italy.
Manufactured in Italy.

10 9 8 7 6 5 4 3 2 1

Library of Congress Cataloging-in-Publication Data

Hoskyns, Barney.
    Beneath the diamond sky: Haight-Ashbury, 1965–1970 / Barney Hoskyns.
        p.   cm.
    Includes index
        1. Haight-Ashbury (San Francisco, Calif.)—History. 2. San
Francisco (Calif.)—History. 3. Haight-Ashbury (San Francisco, Calif.)—Social
life and customs. 4. San Francisco (Calif.)—Social life and customs.
5. Subculture—California—San Francisco—History—20th century.   I. Title.
F869.S36H354   1997   97–19790 CIP
979.4'61—dc21
ISBN 0-684-84180-0

CONTENTS

PAGE 9
PROLOGUE
WE BUILT THIS CITY
ON ROCK'N'ROLL

PAGE 21
CHAPTER 1
RED DOG
THE MATRIX OF THE SOUND
PUTTING IT TO THE TEST
TRIPPING THE SWITCH

PAGE 103
CHAPTER 2
ORANGE SUNSHINE
GRADUATION DAY
BE SURE TO WEAR SOME
FLOWERS IN YOUR HAIR
SUMMER OF LOVE
DEATH OF HIPPIE

PAGE 167
CHAPTER 3
PURPLE HAZE
CHILDREN OF THE FUTURE
TAKING YOU HIGHER
LUV'N'HAIGHT

PAGE 222
BIBLIOGRAPHY
INDEX
AND
ACKNOWLEDGMENTS

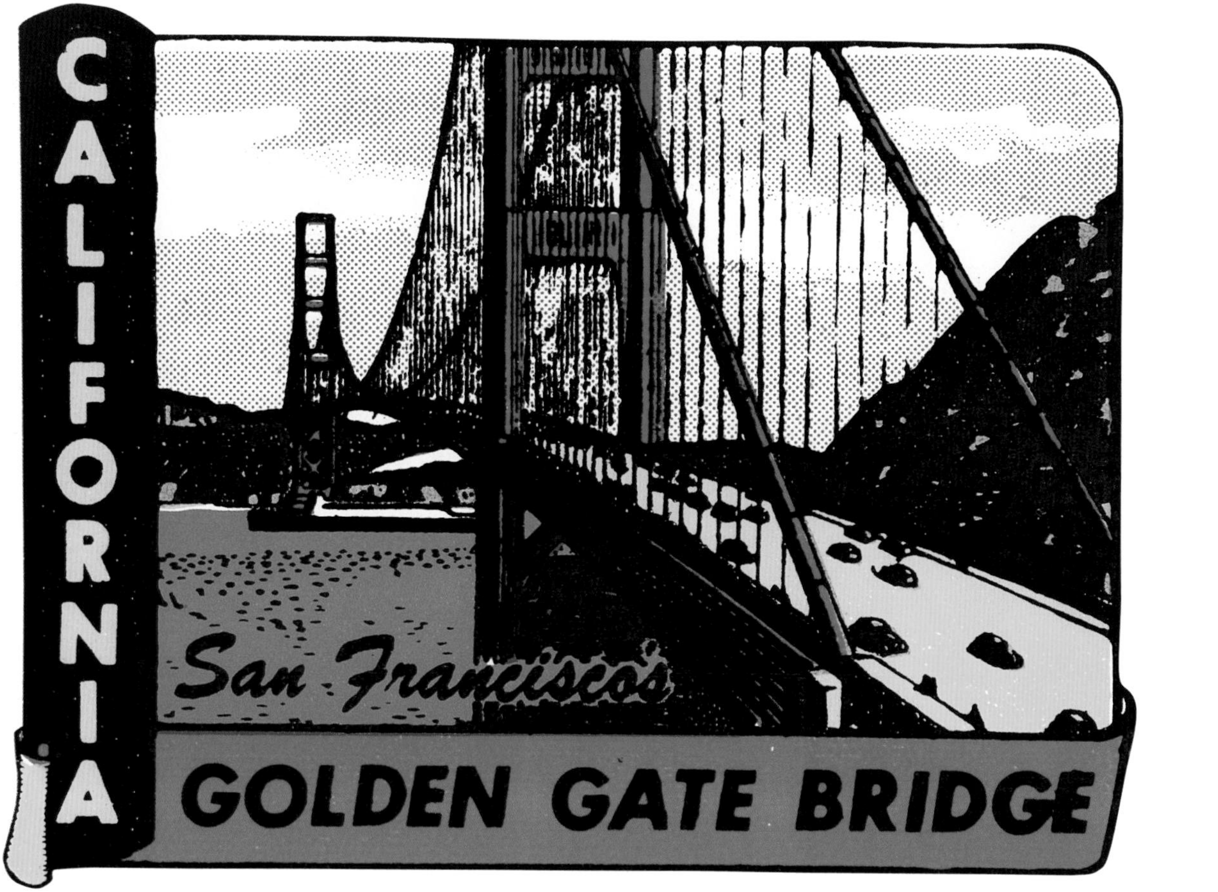
CALIFORNIA
San Francisco's
GOLDEN GATE BRIDGE

We Built This City on

Rock 'n' Roll

"Shall we go, you and I, while we can . . .
Through the transitive nightfall of diamonds?"
THE GRATEFUL DEAD

E A R L Y   I N   J A N U A R Y **1 9 6 3**,
T W O   Y O U N G   T E X A N S   M A D E   A N
E X H A U S T I N G   F O U R - D A Y
J O U R N E Y   F R O M   A U S T I N   T O
S A N   F R A N C I S C O,
driving to that fabled city in search of boho adventures and beatnik glory.
One was a tall, reddish-blond boy; the other a short, unprepossessing girl
with bad skin and a raspy singing voice. They shared a love of folk
ballads and methamphetamine, and they wanted to sample whatever the
city's famed North Beach neighborhood had left to offer.

Janis Lyn Joplin sang in North Beach the very night she arrived,
grabbing an open-mic spot at Coffee and Confusion on Upper Grant
Street. Chester "Chet" Helms, who'd go on to become one of the hippie
kingpins of the San Francisco live music scene, sat and listened to her
as he'd listened at Threadgill's so many times back in Austin. For both
of them, San Francisco must have seemed a golden, Edenic place—a
city at once quaint and freaky, civilized and tolerant of bohemian
deviation; a city where the Beats had settled, where Neal and Carolyn

Cassady had shacked up with Kerouac, where Ginsberg had written *Howl,* where Ferlinghetti had opened his City Lights bookstore. Frisco was the final destination of *On the Road,* dammit: What more did anyone need to know? A city by a bay, with gingerbread mansions packed together on precipitous hills, and sea breezes and thick fogs coming in off the ocean. An antidote to the gasoline Babylon of Los Angeles and the Wall Street Moloch of Manhattan. A small city of European grace, a town middle America could be proud of.

Even this was only half the story, because San Francisco had a pretty *louche* past as a port where sailors and silver prospectors had blown their money on booze and whores and opium dens. "San Francisco is a sailor's town, always was, always will be," wrote Hank Harrison in *The Dead.* "No way to erase the salt from the streets; no way to wipe away the blood." A place, too, where criminals and movie stars loved to live it up. After the Fatty Arbuckle scandal of 1921, when a girl died after having a bottle inserted into her vagina, the San Francisco *Examiner* proclaimed that "Hollywood Must Stop Using San Francisco For A Garbage Can" and demanded that steps be taken to prevent the city being made "the rendezvous for the debauchee and the gangster." The tension between San Francisco's picturesqueness and its hedonism, between its culture and its dissipation, was one that would be played out throughout the Sixties—throughout the rest of Janis Lyn Joplin's life.

"We were just interested in being beatniks then," Joplin reminisced to a *Village Voice* reporter in 1968. "Now we've got responsibilities and, I guess you could say, ambition." In the five years between the singer's arrival in North Beach and the release of her band Big Brother and the Holding Company's first album, *Cheap Thrills,* San Francisco was transformed from a beatnik outpost into a pioneering pop metropolis, a

> Even before the Haight had its day, San Francisco was "a city at once quaint and freaky, civilized and tolerant of bohemian deviation."

place that profoundly and permanently altered the landscape of rock'n'roll and made huge stars out of kids who'd supported each other through lean times in folk clubs and coffeehouses from San José to Sausalito.

Far from the industry centers of New York and L.A., San Francisco was a place where diverse cultural streams threaded together and produced a thrilling, hallucinogenic, multimediated music scene—a place where folk ballads and campus politics and Beat poetics and Prankster happenings and lysergic acid interacted and spontaneously exploded, throwing up a uniquely American form of acid rock that dissolved barriers between bands and audiences and briefly fostered a sense of "community" in the city's rundown Haight-Ashbury neighborhood that may never have been equalled anywhere in the Western world. "The music was somehow always the center of it," says Greg Shaw, who launched the pioneering San Francisco pop fanzine *Mojo Navigator* as a sixteen-year-old in 1965. "It was pretty goofy compared to the records coming out of L.A., but drugs made it seem much better. Really it was just the next evolution of that bohemian lifestyle rather than some pop phenomenon." Along with Janis and Big Brother came Jefferson Airplane, the Grateful Dead, Quicksilver Messenger Service, Country Joe and the Fish, Moby Grape, the Charlatans, and a host of other, lesser or unluckier, entities. The bigger ones broke through to national and international consciousness, setting the pace for the psychedelic overhaul of pop sound and pop style, pushing rock'n'roll into realms of carnival and bacchanal where it had never before ventured—and where it would never truly venture again.

Or would it? The persistence of psychedelia as both a tool and a motif in rock culture is hard to ignore when you look around at the mass Techno gatherings of the Nineties. When British writer Jon

Previous page: A 1962 Grant Avenue street fair—the shape of things to come?

Surveying the hangers-out in a North Beach bagel shop.

15

Savage went to a rave at London's Brixton Academy in the summer of 1993, he noted that "the whole scene reminds me of the place I wanted to be when I was 18: San Francisco's Avalon Ballroom...the sound is Techno, but psychedelic references abound in the light shows, the fashions, the T-shirts reading 'Feed Your Head,' the polydrug use..." The entranced and Ecstatic dancers who lose themselves in the pulsing synthetic rhythms of Orbital and the Chemical Brothers are chasing exactly the same state of bliss or *kairos* that drew the first Deadheads in the San Francisco ballrooms of the mid-Sixties. Guitar-based bands as different as Spiritualized, Mercury Rev, Gorky's Zygotic Mynci, Olivia Tremor Control, and the one-man Bevis Frond incorporate psychedelic and cosmic-rock elements into their sound. Records such as Spectrum's *Songs for Owsley* (referring to the legendary acid baron Owsley Stanley III) even make explicit the debt to the Haight scene. Then there are the many groups who draw directly on the San Francisco sound, whether it's the British group Kula Shaker and their "Grateful When You're Dead/Jerry Was There" or the Japanese outfit White Heaven, who meticulously recreate the Quicksilver-style acid rock of that long-gone time. And let's not forget the whole nomadic, neo-Deadhead scene which has sprung up around American acts like Phish, Rusted Root, and God Street Wine. Mind expansion is clearly not something that's going to go away.

The legendary street corner where it all began.

Was it all just about drugs, then? Or is that the wrong question? Surely the drugs and the music were symbiotically twinned, part and parcel of the same trip, a dual means of breaking down the barriers which had blocked the psyche of American youth for so long. What happened in San Francisco was a grand experiment in quasi-communal living, an attempt to break away from mainstream America—from conformity to capitalist consumerism, from the rigidity of sexual roles,

from the violence of the Vietnam War—and create a new tribe of "beautiful dropouts." Hallucinogenics simply served as the gateway to a new paradise in which the world could be apprehended mystically as a cosmic web rather than as an atomistic rat race.

The experiment failed, of course, and its failure casts a dark shadow over the subsequent history of pop culture. Why did the Love Generation, of all people, not actually learn to love one another? Why did the Sixties end with Altamont, and Haight-Ashbury wind up as a squalid parade of junkies and muggers? Because innocence will always be abused? Or just because it's human nature to fuck up?

JANIS LYN JOPLIN, of course, never had much truck with the notion of the Haight as hippietopia. *They're frauds, the whole goddamn culture,*" she sneered in the summer of 1970. *"They bitch about brainwashing from their parents and they do the same damn thing."*

Janis Joplin and Chet Helms: Two young Texans in search of boho adventures and beatnik glory.

FOUR MONTHS LATER THE GIRL, THE KOZMIC SOUL QUEEN OF SAN FRANCISCO, WAS **DEAD** OF A HEROIN OVERDOSE.

MIND EXPANSION IS CLEARLY NOT SOMETHING THAT'S GOING TO GO AWAY.

CHAPTER 1
RED DOG

The Matrix of the SOUND

"Nobody ever taught you how to live out in the street…"

BOB DYLAN

ON OCTOBER 13, 1955, ELVIS PRESLEY PLAYED the City Auditorium in Amarillo, Texas—just one of countless stops en route to the hysterical adulation he was to experience after signing to RCA-Victor the following month. The same night, far away in San Francisco, six poets—KENNETH REXROTH, ALLEN GINSBERG, GARY SNYDER, PHIL WHALEN, PHILIP 1 LAMANTIA, AND A TEENAGED MICHAEL McCLURE—read their work at the Six gallery on Fillmore Street, creating

21

such a storm that Jack Kerouac, no less, described the event as "the night of the birth of the San Francisco poetry Renaissance." Ginsberg, a twenty-eight-year-old native New Yorker who'd made San Francisco his adoptive city, gave a reading of his epic, Blakean poem, *Howl*. It was to be a foundation stone of Beat subculture.

In truth, the two events weren't so far apart as moments of resistance to the stifling, desensualized dullness of American life in the Fifties. The readings were as much a part of the dawning culture of rock'n'roll as were Presley's scandalous gyrations—his manner, style, and delivery rooted in black R&B. (It was with good reason that Norman Mailer identified the followers of the Beat generation as "white Negroes.") "This was a time of cold, gray silence," Michael McClure was to write. "But inside the coffee houses of North Beach, poets and friends sensed the atmosphere of liberation…we were restoring the body, with the voice as the extension of the body."

The Beats made North Beach the most exciting boho ghetto in North America, howling and hollering their defiant, Whitmanesque exhortations to anyone who'd listen. They were mostly writers, with a sprinkling of artists and musicians at the fringes, and they mobilized themselves around Allen Ginsberg, Jack Kerouac, and William Burroughs. They got their name from an expression Kerouac picked up from a New York low-lifer who used it as a slang term for beaten-down, or exhausted, though Kerouac would claim that the word also carried connotations of beatitude.

The Beats' soundtrack was the bebop they heard at the Blackhawk and the Jazz Workshop; black musicians were their totemic figures, their noble savages of choice. In February 1957, Kenneth Rexroth and Lawrence Ferlinghetti recited poems to the backing of a live quartet at the Cellar on Green Street, later recording an album for the Fantasy jazz

Allen Ginsberg helped to lead San Francisco's Beat revolution in the Fifties, setting the scene for the Haight era.

label across the Bay in Berkeley. Allen Ginsberg and Gary Snyder looked East, studying the tenets of Buddhism and initiating a trend that would be taken up and half-digested by the Haight-Ashbury hippies a decade later. Satirical comedy found a home in North Beach: The acerbic comic Lenny Bruce had his first major club engagement at Ann's 440 in January 1958, and Mort Sahl and Lord Buckley began gigging at the hungry i and the Purple Onion.

William Burroughs said,

After 1957, ON THE ROAD sold a trillion Levis and a million espresso coffee machines, and also sent countless kids on the road. This was of course in part due to the media, the arch-opportunists. They know a story when they see one, and the Beat movement was a story, and a big one...The Beat literary movement came at exactly the right time and said something that millions of people of all nationalities all over the world were waiting to hear. You can't tell anybody anything he doesn't know already. The alienation, the restlessness, the dissatisfaction were already there waiting when Kerouac pointed out the road.

Hit the road, Jack: Levi's ads and dime-store editions of sacred Beat texts.

The seeds of the Sixties, in other words, were already in the soil. They had put forth shoots in the Paris of the 1890s and the Berlin of the 1920s, and now they were sprouting in London and Liverpool and in New York and Los Angeles. Most colorful of all were the shoots coming through in San Francisco.

By the time Janis Joplin and Chet Helms made their trip to San Francisco in 1963, a new generation of pimply would-be bohemians

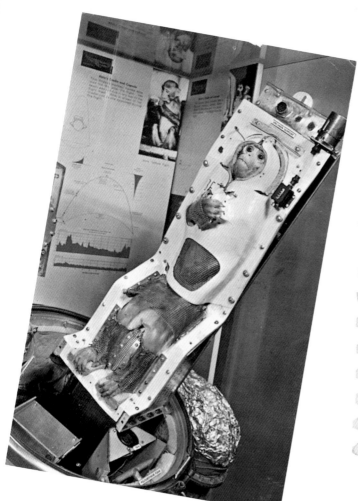

JOHN F. KENNEDY

13c UNITED STATES

In a realm all its own.... *Cadillac*

had begun to frequent North Beach, listening devoutly to folk singers as they sipped their espressos. The Kingston Trio became a more or less permanent fixture at the hungry i. Clubs began opening up all over the Bay Area, luring restless middle-class teens privileged enough to do what no one had had the luxury of doing before: To see through the hollowness of America's consumer society. "I thought I was either going to have to commit suicide or become a bank robber," remembered Jefferson Airplane's Paul Kantner. "I got into folk music and it probably saved my life."

For Kantner, a good Catholic boy who made regular pilgrimages to North Beach from his home in San José, the hungry i and the Blackhawk were "shrines," like the City Lights store and Vesuvio's coffeehouse. "San Francisco has always held a peculiar fascination for people who live outside the pale," he reminisced. "It was like Oz for us, a hedonistic place which gave you the opportunity to be rather flamboyant and extreme in your behavior." Among the kindred souls Kantner would encounter at his "shrines" and elsewhere were several future stars of the San Francisco sound.

Goatee-bearded David Freiberg, later the bass player with Quicksilver Messenger Service, was one half of the folkie duo David and Michela. Kanter's Airplane colleague Jorma (then Jerry) Kaukonen already enjoyed a fearsome reputation as a fingerpicking guitarist by the time he started backing Janis Joplin at his Santa Clara club The Shelter in that summer of 1963. Peter Albin, later of Big Brother, not only sang with his brother Rod in the Liberty Hall Aristocrats, but played blues with a sixteen-year-old Ron (later Pigpen) McKernan. Jerry Garcia performed in the Wildwood Boys with David Nelson and Robert Hunter, future lyricist of the Grateful Dead. Says Kantner, "There was a great intermix of people weaving in and

Symbols of a new dawn: JFK, the Cadillac, and the first monkey in space.

27

... AND THE GLOW FROM THAT FIRE CAN TRULY LIGHT THE WORLD ·

U.S. POSTAGE

5c

1917 · JOHN FITZGERALD KENNEDY · 1963

out of each other's lives that was very intriguing and very entrancing and always interesting."

"I think one of the major significant points about early San Francisco music lay in the traditional orientation of the musicians," noted Robert Hunter. "Just about everyone hit rock music via an extensive folk background." Reared on The Weavers and Pete Seeger, the new folkies would play hoot nights at the Drinking Gourd on Union Street—or the Tangent down in Palo Alto, or the Off Stage in San José, or wherever it might be—trying their hands at traditional tunes or at Dino Valenti's new song "Get Together." Over coffee, huddled in duffelcoats and a fog of cigarette smoke, they would rage about the Bay of Pigs. Then some of them would head back to someone's funky apartment and partake of more illicit smokeables. "It was a group of well-educated children breaking out of bonds set for them that didn't really apply," says Paul Kantner. "And almost, in their own way, throwing themselves into a fire of unknown origin. Grace [Slick] once mentioned that our generation had no challenges...so we sort of took it upon ourselves to challenge ourselves."

The death of JFK on November 22, 1963, remains a sixties benchmark.

Busy challenging themselves down in the affluent peninsula suburb of Menlo Park were Jerry Garcia and Robert Hunter. Garcia's background was fairly exotic anyway, but nothing like the scenes he witnessed when he gatecrashed parties at the cottage of novelist Ken Kesey near Stanford University. Despite the pair's essential seriousness about music—particularly the bluegrass songs that obsessed Garcia, who by 1963 was a highly accomplished banjo player—both were open to the new world of drugs. Indeed, Hunter, like Kesey himself, was busy playing guinea-pig in a series of infamous drug experiments at the local Veterans' Hospital.

Kesey had been told about the experiments—among them trials of

"psychomimetic" drugs that temporarily replicated psychoses—by psychology student Vic Lovell. The good drugs were mindblasting, and king of them all was lysergic acid diathylamide—LSD or "acid."—synthesized in 1938 by Swiss chemist Albert Hoffmann as a possible cure for migraine.

Kesey, thirty-one, married with three children, had already begun to assert himself as the charismatic ringleader of an anarchic post-beatnik scene around Palo Alto. A rugged, curly-haired farm boy from Oregon, he had arrived at Stanford University on a creative-writing fellowship in 1958, later moving into the artsy-boho enclave that was Perry Lane and helping himself to samples of LSD and mescaline during the Veterans' Hospital tests. It was while working as a night attendant on the hospital's psych ward that he conceived the idea for *One Flew Over the Cuckoo's Nest.*

Coffeehouse culture in the early Sixties: "A group of well-educated children breaking out of bonds that didn't apply anymore."

In the fall of 1961 Neal Cassady, Beat legend and inspiration for Kerouac's Dean Moriarty in *On the Road,* pitched up at Perry Lane and proceeded to become a kind of aide-de-camp to Kesey. Cassady, then about thirty-five in 1961, had been an *éminence grise* for Kerouac and Ginsberg. But both men had moved on, and Cassady was looking for a new Master. His chief loves were cars and girls: He claimed that by age twenty-one he'd stolen five hundred cars and slept with 750 women. Unlike Kerouac and Ginsberg, he was from a poor, dispossessed background. Apparently owing allegiance to no one, he had outsider credibility in spades, and embodied the spirit of the Beats for everyone who consorted with him.

At Kesey's Perry Lane cottage formidable amounts of hallucinogenics were consumed by both occupants and the growing number of writers, artists, and general liggers who would show up there. "We were younger

CAN **YOU** PASS THE ACID TEST ?

than most of the Pranksters [as the core group later became known]," remembered Jerry Garcia, who was among the more tentative of the Perry Lane regulars. "We weren't serious college people. We were on the street. We just got high and went crazy, you know? Socially, our scene had a little bit of the kids of Stanford alumni and faculty. It was in Palo Alto, which is more bohemian than anything else. But we were definitely Dionysian."

In the summer of 1963, royalties from the acclaimed *Cuckoo's Nest*—which was later made into a famous movie starring Jack Nicholson—paid for a big log house in the hills of La Honda, northwest of Palo Alto. Here Kesey and his compadres really went for it: Isolated within six acres in a mountain creek, they were free to pursue their chemical experiments out of eyesight and earshot, wiring up equipment and speakers in the house and in the redwoods surrounding it so they could groove to Rahsaan Roland Kirk records while chopping wood. Kesey gradually began to abandon writing, seeing it as an essentially reductive and bourgeois exercise and instead embracing something altogether more primordial and existential.

The Pranksters rattled across America in this 1939 International Harvester bus.

Everything now came down to the crucial experience of LSD, which made it impossible to continue to live by the straight world's games. When Kesey's tough, larger-than life pal Ken Babbs returned from active duty as a helicopter pilot in Vietnam, the Merry Pranksters were born, and things became rapidly more intense and maniacal. The Pranksters bought a 1939 International Harvester school bus which had already done service for a family man who'd adapted it for the use of his eleven offspring (with bunks and benches and a sink and so forth), and daubed it with psychedelic swirls and patterns and endowed it with intense spiritual significance. The bus was to become a center and a symbol for the Pranksters: You were either on it or off it, cosmically speaking. The

Pranksters embarked in the summer of 1964 on an insane, sleepless, paranoid odyssey that took them all the way through the deserts of the Southwest to Texas and New Orleans and then up to New York City for the publication of Kesey's second opus, *Sometimes a Great Notion,* all the while filming their escapades and encounters with straight America. At the rear of the bus hung a sign: CAUTION: WEIRD LOAD; at the front, its destination board read: FURTHUR—with two "u"s.

Upon reaching New York, Kesey and Babbs sat on top of the bus with flutes and whistles and played music to match the look of the people on the street—sad, aggressive, resentful, nervous, drunk, whatever. It was a measure of just how far the Pranksters had gone that when they made an unscheduled and unannounced visit to Millbrook, New York, to call in on acid gurus Timothy Leary and Richard Alpert, they were deemed too chaotic and too rambunctious to fit in with the so-called League for Spiritual Discovery. For their part they found Leary and Alpert, authors of the just-published *The Psychedelic Experience,* altogether too solemn and precious about the business of psychedelic liberation. The Pranksters decried the gulf between this overly intellectual, fundamentally old-world scene, and what was starting to happen back home on the West Coast.

Neil Cassady, Beat luminary and model for Kerouac's Dean Moriarty.

Acid changed everything in San Francisco, and the Pranksters were evangelical to the point of zealotry in their attempts to turn people onto it. "Nobody was on any spiritual quest back then," recalled Ellen Harmon, a partner of Chet Helms' in the concert-promotion collective known as the Family Dog. "What it was, was getting away from mother and father so you could do whatever you wanted—which, in most cases, was just lying around and getting as high as you could! Then what happened was, everybody took a bunch of acid and got all *wired.* That's

what happened to the scene! They got serious!" Acid was a dividing line between the old and the new, between the old Beat scene and the new youth counterculture. Beat veterans used the pejorative term "hippies"—ironically a term black musicians coined for white beatnik hangers-on in the jazz scene—to describe middle-class kids slumming it in North Beach, but it only betrayed how threatened they felt now that they were no longer running the show. Change was in the air, and the folkies who were in their early twenties knew they had to establish their own scene.

With North Beach becoming expensively gentrified, a number of coffeehouses and hip clothing stores began to open in Haight-Ashbury, a blue-collar, ethnically mixed neighborhood east of Golden Gate Park that was also home to students from the creative hotbed of San Francisco State University. The Blue Unicorn coffeehouse opened in early 1964, and by the summer "hippies" were shedding traditional beatnik garb and wearing the crazier clothes they found in funky emporia like Peggy Caserta's Mnasidika and Mike Ferguson's Magic Theater for Madmen Only. (The Magic Theater may have been the city's first bona fide head shop: Opened in 1961 by Mike Ferguson, who would soon be playing piano in the seminal Charlatans, it specialized in dope pipes and musty Edwardian garments. In the succinct words of Charlatans' founder George Hunter, "The Magic Theater was the signature element in terms of a unifying force for the post-beatnik/pre-hippie people.")

The new styles of flowing locks and robes went hand in hand with the new acid consciousness. Just as Albert Hoffmann had experienced "an uninterrupted stream of fantastic pictures, extraordinary shapes with an intense, kaleidoscopic play of colors" after first synthesizing LSD-25, so the Haight's new psychedelic disciples were seeing the world

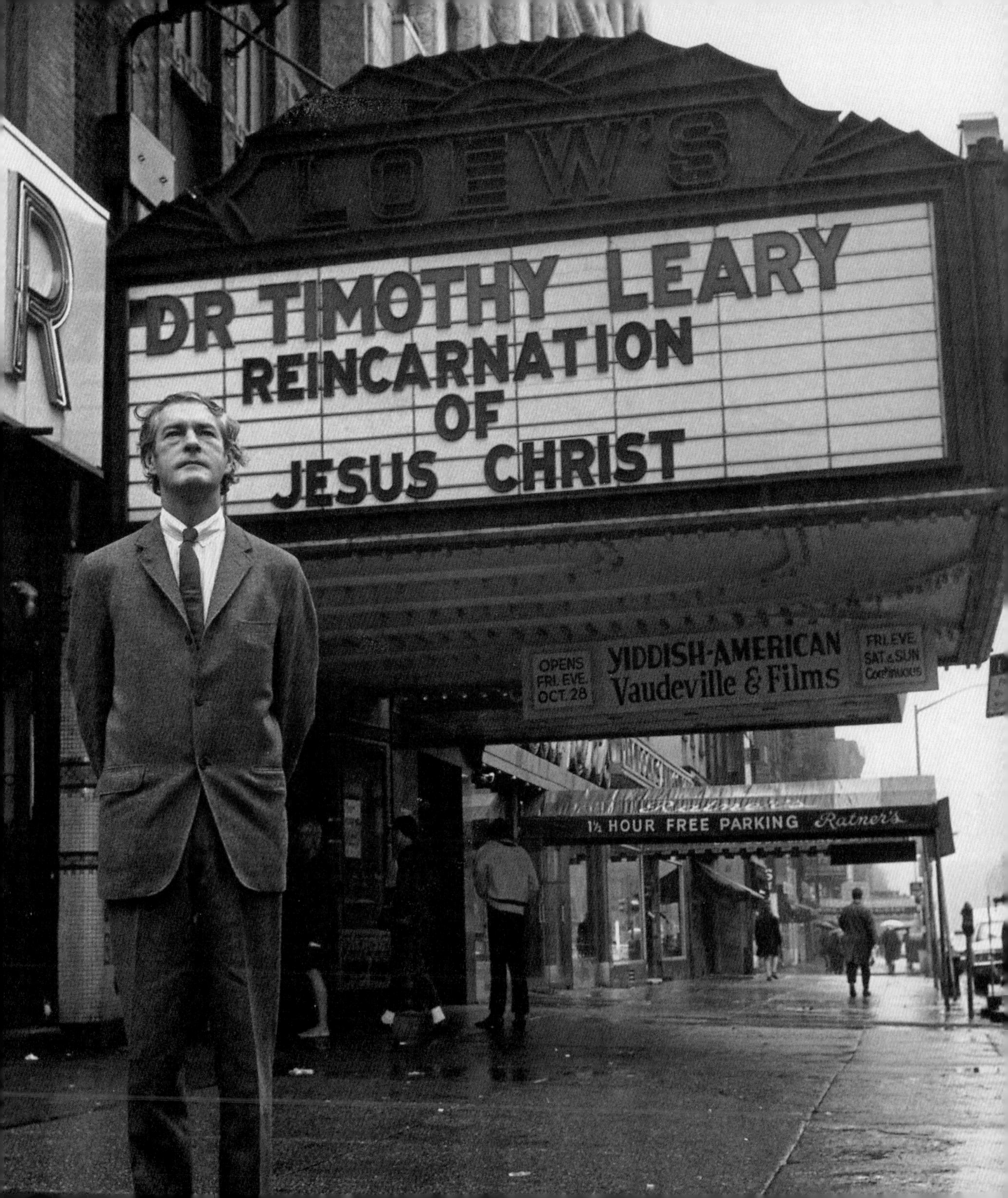
LOEW'S
DR TIMOTHY LEARY
REINCARNATION
OF
JESUS CHRIST
OPENS FRI. EVE. OCT. 28
YIDDISH-AMERICAN
Vaudeville & Films
FRI. EVE. SAT. & SUN Continuous
1½ HOUR FREE PARKING Ratner's

anew, casting off clothes and attitudes that had acted like straitjackets through their repressed adolescences. Life in the Haight took on a zany, freaky, anarchic quality.

Contemporaneous with these mini-revolutions in everyday life was the new sound of electric rock'n'roll, breaking free of sanctimonious folk protest songs on the one hand and sappy, vapid teenypop on the other. Spearheading rock's revolution were the Beatles, whose hits initially met with scorn on the Bay Area folk circuit but were now making the hippier contingent rethink their stance. With the new wave of British invasion bands taking America by storm, and even Bob Dylan flirting with the ghost of electricity, folkies defected en masse. "The Beatles came along and that was pretty much it," noted Darby Slick of the Great Society. "Folk music just went instantly into the dumper." Slowly, as 1964 turned into 1965, acid began to penetrate pop. By December '65, *Rubber Soul* was the Haight's soundtrack.

Down in Palo Alto, Jerry Garcia had seen the light. Early in 1965 he and Ron McKernan went the whole way and put together what was essentially an electric R&B outfit, playing covers that were already staples of British groups. "Basically we got our first gigs because we were a blues-oriented Rolling Stones-style band," Garcia recalled later. "There were sound musicological reasons why psychedelic music happened," Barry Melton of Country Joe and the Fish told *Guitar Player*. "Rather than being some drug-induced thing, it was really a bunch of serious folkie musicologists who played blues and bluegrass joining forces with guys who played at the edge of town, chewed gum and couldn't put two sentences together—the rock and roll players."

The first show by the Warlocks, as they were christened, took place in May, 1965, at Magoo's Pizza Parlor in Menlo Park, with Bobby Weir on guitar, Billy Kreutzmann on drums, and Dana Morgan, Jr., son of the

For the Pranksters, Timothy Leary was altogether too precious about the business of psychedelic liberation.

local guitar store owner, on bass. Booking agent Al King quickly got them other dates: Bars in Redwood City and the East Bay, stripjoints on Broadway in North Beach. Bluegrass diehards couldn't believe Garcia was in a band that was playing "Money" and "Gloria" and "In The Midnight Hour," but after all the studious seriousness of the bluegrass scene Garcia was having a ball.

Two things set the Warlocks apart from a multitude of similar outfits: They could actually play, and they looked different—Garcia like a hairy freak, McKernan like a greasy biker. Billy Kreutzmann was one of the best drummers on the scene, and Garcia was close to mastering the electric guitar. The only weak link—Dana Morgan, Jr.—was soon ditched in favor of Phil "Professor" Lesh, a College of San Mateo graduate who'd studied with the avant-garde composer Luciano Berio; he played his first Warlocks gig at Frenchy's in Fremont in July '65. Garcia quickly saw where Lesh's musicianship and erudition could take them. "He had the best musical education, a music major. He took me over to his apartment in Berkeley, and there he was with a card table and no piano. He was writing a piece for three orchestras out of his head, with no piano. I couldn't fucking believe it."

Others were seeing the light, too. In the Haight, a blond southern California boy who'd followed his girlfriend up to the Bay Area was putting the finishing touches to his band the Charlatans at San Francisco State. George Hunter wasn't studying at the university, but he was the hippest guy around the campus, the cat with the longest hair and the freakiest ideas. Influenced as much by the paintings of Maxfield Parrish as by the music of the Rolling Stones, he conceived the idea of a band playing blues and country-folk songs and wearing the kind of Edwardian gear that was becoming popular around the Haight. After meeting bass player Richie Olsen through his girlfriend, Hunter literally

Pop's mind expands: By December '65, *Rubber Soul* was the Haight's soundtrack.

Overleaf: The Solidarity Day march from Washington, D.C.

41

designed the band in the way he designed architectural models.

The pieces came together slowly. Mike Wilhelm was a folk guitarist Hunter had known at Canoga Park High in Los Angeles and who'd shown up at the Blue Unicorn; drummer Dan Hicks was an S.F. State student who'd majored in radio and TV and shown up at Hunter's apartment looking for pot; pianist Mike Ferguson was the proprietor of the Magic Theater for Madmen Only. "Hunter had a pretty difficult task," guitarist Mike Wilhelm told Alec Palao. "He had the concept, and then he had to keep modifying it to fit what he actually had." The first lineup, in homage to William Burroughs, was called the Mainliners, but changed its name to the Charlatans because that was essentially what Hunter was—a poseur in love with the idea of being in a rock'n'roll band, unable to sing or play an instrument.

The early Charlatans. From left: Richie Olsen, Mike Wilhelm, George Hunter, Mike Ferguson, Sam Linde.

In the summer of 1965, a man sporting the colorful appellation "Travis T. Hip" (real name Chandler Laughlin) came to San Francisco in search of a house band for a renovated saloon in the old silver mining town of Virginia City, Nevada, a three-hour drive from the Bay Area. He'd been sent by Mark Unobsky, a trust-fund kid from Memphis who'd bought the abandoned Virginia City gambling hall with the notion of creating a modern-day Wild West scene in the town. The timing couldn't have been better. Introduced to Hunter by painter and light-show pioneer Bill Ham, Laughlin took one look at the band in their thrift-store, dandy-outlaw finery and invited them to Virginia City. They had never actually played a gig.

An insane, acid-impaired audition at the newly named Red Dog Saloon did not deter Unobsky from hiring the Charlatans, who had developed a repertoire of songs like "Alabama Bound" and "Wabash Cannonball" in an effort to distance themselves from the British Invasion sound. Mixed up with blues evergreens like Robert Johnson's

"32-20" and quirky Dan Hicks songs like "How Can I Miss You When You Won't Go Away," these numbers were enough to pack people in on weekends through the summer. Among the people who came to check out the band were a number of very significant visitors from San Francisco itself: People like Darby Slick, John Cipollina, and future poster artist Rick Griffin, along with Chet Helms, Ellen Harmon, and Alton Kelley of the Family Dog. This contingent more than made up for the hostility the Charlatans would periodically encounter from local rednecks, though perhaps not for the close shaves they experienced in a town that had become seriously trigger-happy. The band themselves was armed at all times for the three and a half months of their Red Dog residency: It was the only way to ensure any respect as longhaired hippie boys.

George Hunter's poster —a.k.a. "The Seed"—for the Charlatans' legendary residency at the Red Dog.

Summer '65 also saw the formation of the Jefferson Airplane, born after Marty Balin approached Paul Kantner one night at the Drinking Gourd with the proposal that they start a band. Balin, a former member of folk group the Town Criers, had heard the Byrds' "MR. TAMBOURINE MAN" while he was in Los Angeles and come "beetling back" to San Francisco in order to put together a similar kind of folk-rock group. Kantner, now living in a Fillmore commune with his girlfriend Ginger Jackson and with David Freiberg, needed little persuading of the merits of amplification. Together they recruited the remaining members of the band: Bassist Bob Harvey, acclaimed guitarist Jerry/Jorma Kaukonen, singer Signe Toly, and a drummer—or at least a guitar player who "looked like" a drummer—by the name of Skip Spence.

Hastily they developed an electrified repertoire of songs like Judy Henske's "High Flying Bird" and Fred Neil's "The Other Side Of This Life." Balin persuaded a friend and his roommates to buy a pizza parlor

Overleaf: The Beats had already made North Beach the most exciting boho ghetto in North America. From left: An informal reading by Michael Grieg; audience at a poetry event at Fugizi Hall; Lawrence Ferlinghetti at the Jazz Cellar; the lights of the famous Colt Tower.

on Fillmore Street in order to turn it into a club, and the Matrix opened on Friday, August 13, 1965. Before long, word about the Airplane had spread as far as the offices of the San Francisco *Chronicle,* where the veteran jazz critic Ralph J. Gleason was keeping close tabs on the nascent pop scene. A Gleason review described the band somewhat Germanically as "a contemporary-popular-music-folk-rock unit," and it was enough to get the attention of a few record companies, as well as of a rather sinister-looking manager, Matthew Katz, who'd lurked on the periphery of the folk scene for some years. Within weeks, Katz was representing the group. The music of the Airplane, like that of the Warlocks and the Charlatans, was the matrix of

The Jefferson Airplane takes flight. From left: Jack Casady, Spencer Dryden, Paul Kantner, Marty Balin, Signe Toly Anderson, Jorma Kaukonen.

the new sound of San Francisco: Psychedelic blues, electric folk, cosmic country rock, call it what you will. Matthew Katz called it "FOJAZZ."

Putting It to the Test

AS PSYCHEDELIC ROCK DAWNED IN THE HAIGHT, a host of independent record labels formed in the Bay Area, most of them catering to the more **MAINSTREAM DEMAND FOR BRITISH INVASION-STYLE POP MUSIC.** One crucial step ahead of them was Autumn, formed by a pair of colorful deejays who, in 1961, had fled the payola scandal in their native Philadelphia and joined the San Francisco Top 40 station KYA.

Tom "Big Daddy" Donahue and Bobby "Mighty Mitch" Mitchell were now major players on the scene, having promoted a series of giant teen "revues" (starring the likes of the Beach Boys and the Righteous Brothers) at venues such as the 18,000-seat Cow Palace. Hiring twenty-one-year-old Sylvester "Sly" Stewart, a brilliant multi-instrumentalist from the rough industrial East Bay town of Vallejo, they formed Cougar Productions as a vehicle for him, then launched Autumn.

The label's first hit—going Top 5 in August, 1964—was the novelty-dance track "C'mon And Swim" by Bobby Freeman, the singer who'd scored San Francisco's first big rock'n'roll hit "Do You Wanna Dance?" in 1958. Other R&B and soul sides followed, but it wasn't until a hooker recommended that Donahue and Mitchell check out the Beau Brummels at a club in San Mateo that they followed up Freeman's success. The Brummels were shameless Beatles imitators, but S.F. State graduate Ron Elliott wrote great songs and Sal Valentino was a hell of a singer.

53

With Sly at the controls, they cut "Laugh Laugh," a strong folk-rock number in a Searchers vein that made the Top 20 in early 1965. Within a few months, Donahue and Mitchell had signed a bunch of other teen-rock acts: The Tikis, the Mojo Men, the Knight Riders, and the Vejtables.

As a pre-hippie, pre-acid rock label, Autumn wasn't really so different from the kind of indie companies which were emerging in Los Angeles. They signed and released sides by bands who would end up looking hopelessly square next to the more out-there Haight-Ashbury groups, but that shouldn't discount their achievement in laying the groundwork for San Francisco as a music industry town. "The whole local scene began with the Beau Brummels and the Vejtables, it didn't begin with the Airplane," says Cyril Jordan of the Flamin' Groovies, another San Francisco band who would never quite make the grade in the Haight.

Tom "Big Daddy" Donahue, renegade disc jockey and co-founder of Autumn Records.

"Autumn was the perfect example of what was going on then," says David Rubinson, a Columbia Records staff producer from New York who'd produced live albums at the hungry i and even worked with the Mime Troupe. "Hippies trying to do business, businessmen trying to be hippies." Donahue and Mitchell also had the savvy, in July, 1965, to open America's first real "pschedelic discotheque," Mother's, described nicely by Gene Sculatti as a "pulsating ultraviolet cavern doing weird business along the topless Broadway sin-strip in North Beach."

An oft-overlooked aspect of Bay Area music history is the countless teen-rock/garage-punk bands who played in San Francisco's suburbs in the mid-Sixties—overlooked because they were deemed to be unoriginal and because of an innate urban snobbery toward the city's outlying neighborhoods. This "punk" rock was essentially Anglophile in style and demeanor, and its Vox-organ-and-tambourine sound was undeniably formulaic. Many of the groups were strongly influenced by Paul Revere and the Raiders, cranking out R&B and fuzz-punk

66% /.
41% c.

BANDS!

THE MYSTERY TREND

THE SYNDICATE OF SOUND

THE CHOCOLATE WATCHBAND

WILLIAM PENN & HIS PALS

THE MOJO MEN

instrumentals in their matching American Revolution outfits. "The excitement people felt for our group was really just a spinoff of the excitement people felt for the Beatles and Stones," was the humble admission of Mike Shapiro, whose band William Penn and his Pals also featured the pre-Santana voice and keyboard playing of a young Gregg Rolie.

The Chocolate Watch Band hailed from San José, starting out as a Stonsey covers band playing teen-rock venues like the Bold Knight in Sunnyvale and Winchester Cathedral in Redwood City. Singer Dave Aguilar was an almost uncanny Mick Jagger copyist, as a song like "Don't Need Your Lovin'" demonstrates, but occasionally—as on the brilliant "No Way Out"—the band came closer to what was happening in the Haight. Santa Clara's Syndicate of Sound auditioned the classic "Little Girl" for a bored Sly Stone, and couldn't even get the record played on San Francisco radio when it was first released locally on the tiny Hush label. Only after garnering airplay in San José did the song, picked up by Bell in New York, climb all the way to No. 8 on the charts.

"There were three different scenes in San Francisco," recalled Cyril Jordan of the Groovies. "The Bill Graham/Chet Helms scene; the underground scene, like us; and then the Vejtables, the Mojo Men, the Beau Brummels...there were these three levels and none of these groups could go into the next level and work. I don't know why, but there's a horrible pecking order in this town." Mike Shapiro of William Penn and his Pals remembered playing a show in Petaluma with the Grateful Dead and going to say hello: "The difference between their dressing room and ours was incredible. They had women with beads and jugs of wine, smoking pot—people walking around without their clothes on."

Somewhat artier than the suburban garage-punk bands were two

Bay Area garage-punk bands who fell by the wayside. Clockwise from top: The Mystery Trend, the Chocolate Watchband, the Mojo Men, William Penn and his Pals, the Syndicate of Sound.

groups who formed at San Francisco State, that hotbed of early Sixties' experimentation. Briefly hip with the burgeoning Haight crowd, the Mystery Trend's basic lack of interest in drugs eventually counted against them. "I thought all that psychedelic shit was a lot of crap," singer-organist Ron Nagle reflected later. "We did not embrace the brotherly love trip." Equally hostile to the love crowd were the Final Solution, formed at S.F. State by Ernie Fosselius and Bob Knickerbocker. "We had this weird unsophisticated dislike for the scene," remembered Fosselius. "We dressed in black head to foot, tried not to smile, smoked a lot, tried to look as emaciated as possible…we were really punks." Then, as now, "punk rock" was the sworn enemy of hippie culture.

Looking back thirty years, it is possible to imagine a parallel pop universe in which the Warlocks disappear into the mists of time like William Penn and his Pals. What the Warlocks had going for them that the Pals did not, however, was a potent combination of vision, ambition, and self-belief…not to mention an in with Ken Kesey and his Merry Pranksters.

Angels in the Panhandle, Golden Gate Park, 1967.

"One day the idea was there," recalled Jerry Garcia. " "Why don't we have a big party and you guys bring your instruments and play, and us Pranksters'll set up all our tape recorders and bullshit, and we'll all get stoned?" And that was the first Acid Test…right away we dropped completely out of the straight music scene and just played the Tests." Here is the turning point for San Franciscan rock: A band that could theoretically have gone the Top 40/AM Radio/*American Bandstand* route but instead turned away and boldly decided to throw in their lot with a bunch of acid-guzzling renegades in La Honda—renegades, moreover, who by now had been busted for pot and were busy courting the most notorious of all California's subcultural tribes, the Hell's Angels. At a big La Honda party for the Angels on August 7, 1965, the fearsome bikers of

Oakland consorted with such guests as Allen Ginsberg—who, as a Jewish New York intellectual homosexual, must have been close to everything an Angel would abominate—and the new acid superdealer Augustus Owsley Stanley III, source of the purest and the best LSD in the world.

Owsley rejoiced in many nicknames—the Bear, the Naughty Chemist, the White Rabbit—and manufactured millions of tabs of LSD. Some say that he kept his prices low, and even gave away as much as he sold. But he could afford to be generous: When LSD was still legal, he was able to buy a 500-gram consignment of the basic constituent of LSD, lysergic acid monohydrate, for $20,000, and turn it into a-million-and-a-half doses wholesaling at about $1.50 a piece. In Tom Wolfe's words he was "a cocky little guy, short, with dark hair, dressed like an acid head, the usual boho gear, but with a strange wound-up nasal voice…" At the height of his fame he was thirty years old.

Ernie Fosselius' Final Solution rock the Haight. "We were really punks," said Ernie.

The first "Acid Test," if you could even call it that, took place in a somewhat desultory and disorganized manner at Ken Babbs' house in Santa Cruz, in the fall of 1965. "It started off as a party," wrote Tom Wolfe, "with movies flashed on the walls, and lights, and tapes, and the Pranksters providing the music themselves, not to mention the LSD." Wary the Warlocks may have been of Kesey the guru-bully—wary too of the hammer that Neal Cassady kept hurling around the room—but they could see that this anarchic participatory experiment was a long way from Top 40 titty joints on the El Camino Real.

"When it was moving right, you could dig that there was something…like ordered chaos," remembered Jerry Garcia. "Everybody would be high and flashing and going through insane changes during which everything would be demolished…so there would be this odd interchange going on, electroneural connections of weird sorts." The

Warlocks' decision to become a sort of house band for the Acid Tests, and in the process change their name to the Grateful Dead, was one of the key events in the evolution of the San Francisco scene. Equally important was their decision to attend the second dance staged by Chet Helms' Family Dog collective on October 24. "What this scene needs is us," muttered an acid-flashing Phil Lesh as he wandered amidst the psychedelic throng at the Longshoremen's Hall.

Chet Helms himself had seen the hallucinogenic light early in '65, when his first acid trip convinced him to stop shooting methamphetamine. With the help of Luria Castell, a veteran of the demonstration/sit-in scene, he managed to wean himself off the stuff and mellow out. (His pal Janis Joplin wasn't so lucky: Dealing speed from a scuzzy rooming house on Geary Street, she had a virtual breakdown in the spring and decided to head home to Texas.) A loose in-crowd of cutting-edge Haight hippies—Ellen Harmon, the Charlatans, artists Alton Kelley and Stanley Mouse, photographer Herb Greene, and future Grateful Dead manager Rock Scully—began to form around Helms and Castell, calling itself the Family Dog.

The Family Dog comes together: Chet Helms in the foreground, the Charlatans to the rear.

One afternoon that summer, Helms was making his rounds in the Haight and decided to stop in on Rod Albin at the huge Victorian mansion that his uncle owned on Page Street. When Albin took him down to see the vast panelled ballroom in the basement, Chet hit on the idea of throwing weekly jam sessions with a band led by Rod and his brother Pete. With a readymade audience of friends from the Dog House commune on nearby Pine Street, a nascent Big Brother & the Holding Company—the Albins plus guitarists Sam Andrew and "Weird" Jim Gurley—began attracting sizeable gatherings to the Wednesday night jams.

Helms, a gentle man whose Christ-like appearance proclaimed his

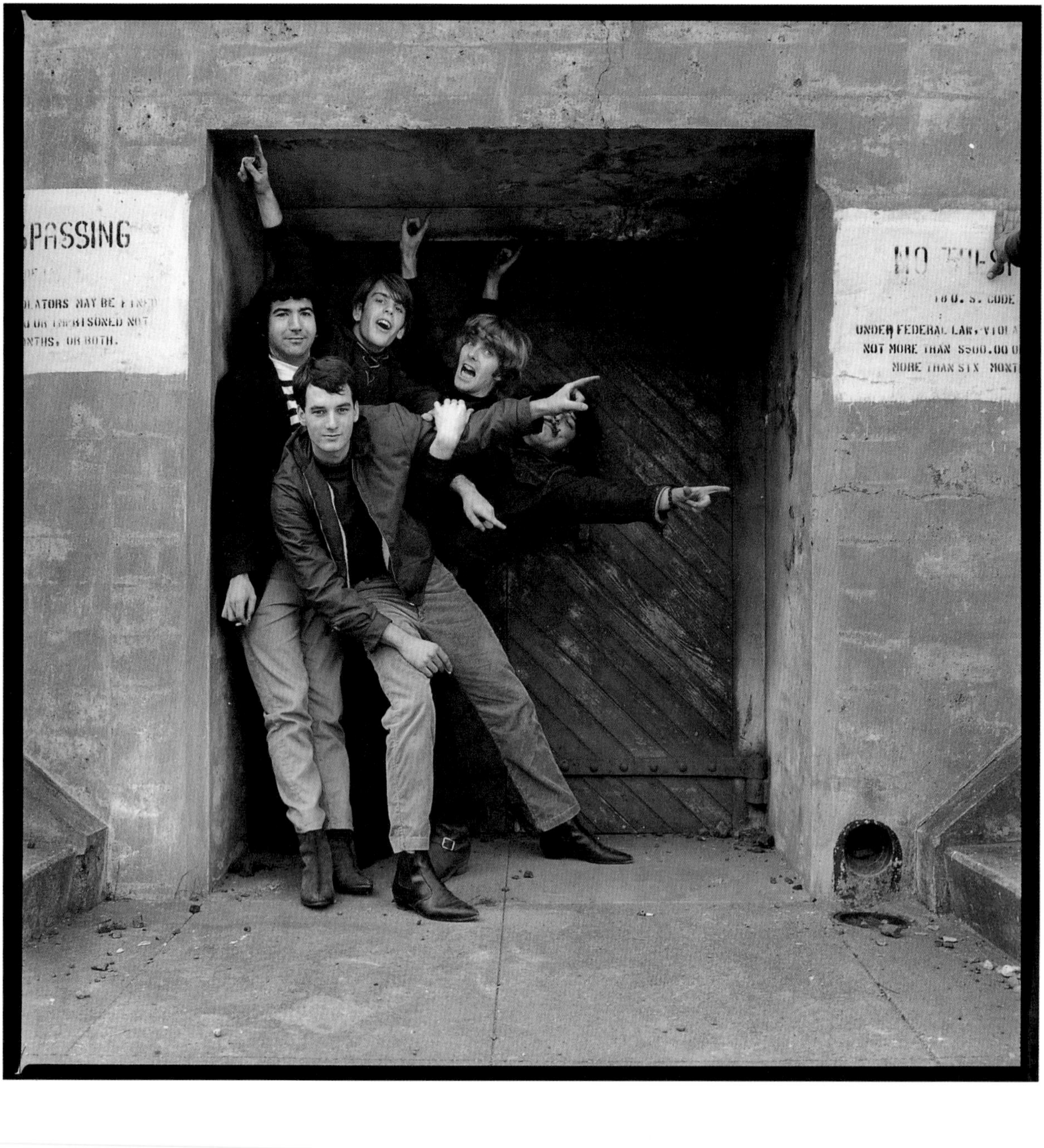

SPASSING
NO
UNDER FEDERAL LAW
NOT MORE THAN
MORE THAN SIX

genuine adhesion to hippie mores, quickly saw the potential of this kind of ballroom gig, and proposed to his fellow Family members that they stage a show in a larger venue. The result was the very first Family Dog dance, the so-called "Tribute to Doctor Strange," an event of incalculable importance held at the Longshoremen's Hall on October 16, 1965, and described by Joel Selvin in his *Summer of Love* as "a subterranean community meeting itself for the first time"—to the sounds of the Jefferson Airplane, the Charlatans, the Great Society, and Oakland's the Marbles.

The Warlocks turn into the Grateful Dead. From left: Jerry Garcia, Bill Kreutzmann, Bob Weir, Phil Lesh, Ron "Pigpen" McKernan.

This is where it all came together: Where the heads crawled out from the woodwork and discovered each other, where the new hippies realized to their amazement that they actually did constitute a community of sorts and did view the world together through the new lenses of acid consciousness. This is where the soaring folk-rock of the Airplane was heard for the first time outside the Matrix, and where the band's future singer Grace Slick made her first real mark with the Great Society. This is where Ralph Gleason—a forty-eight-year-old, cheroot-smoking, jazz journalist—met a pushy young Berkeley student named Jann Wenner, planting the seed that would become *Rolling Stone* magazine; and where John Cipollina met Gary Duncan and Greg Elmore and talked about founding the Quicksilver Messenger Service.

The Family Dog threw two further dances that fall: "A Tribute to Sparkle Plenty," headlined by the Lovin' Spoonful, and "A Tribute to Ming the Merciless," headlined by L.A.'s Mothers of Invention. Memorably described on its poster as "a Wham-bang, wide open stoned DANCE flicking on at dusk," "A tribute to Ming the Merciless" sadly degenerated into a series of ugly brawls—bad vibes all round. Altogether more harmonious was the benefit show for the San Francisco Mime Troupe staged on November 6 by a hyperenergetic

Berlin-born Jewish refugee named Bill Graham.

Now in his mid-thirties, Graham had been born Wolfgang Wolodja Grajanka into a very different world from that of Bay Area. He had lost his parents in the concentration camps, but had himself managed to escape from Nazi Germany as a boy. Hitching from New York, he began visiting San Francisco in the Fifties. For a while he worked as a statistician and a timekeeper, all the while harboring the desire to act or at least become involved with more bohemian endeavors. After bumming around Europe at the turn of the decade, he finally returned to San Francisco and took a job as office manager with heavy equipment firm Allis-Chalmers. Still the theater tugged at him, and he began working on the side as business manager with the Mime Troupe.

At the end of 1964 Graham quit Allis-Chalmers to devote himself full time to what he now considered his vocation—"the carrying out of the details of public assemblage," as he later defined it. By his own admission the Mime Troupe were the first radicals he'd ever met, an anarchic, Pranksterish bunch who specialized in skits and sketches directed against America's stupefied, conscience-less society. Mime Troupe member Peter Berg thought Graham was "really just straight New York, New York Fifties, not Sixties," a square who'd learned his moves on the streets of the Bronx and lacked any ideological empathy with Berg or Troupe founder Ronny Davis. But there was no denying the guy's energy when he organized an appeal to cover Davis' legal fees after the Troupe defied a Parks Commission ruling on staging performances in Lafayette Park.

Graham never forgot the sight of the queue stretching along Howard Street on November 6, 1965, waiting to get into the Mime Troupe loft to see the Jefferson Airplane, the Mystery Trend, the Fugs and others play the appeal. He'd had no idea there were so many of these underground

Bill Graham, Fillmore promoter and warlord of the Bay Area rock scene.

groovers out there, primed for multimedia frolics and rock'n'roll that wasn't just teenage party music. Inside the loft there were films being projected on the walls, and fruit dangled from the ceilings. Booze and acid-spiked Kool-Aid were dispensed from garbage cans lined with aluminum foil. From New York, the Fugs perpetrated their own Lower East Side brand of satirical/scatological outrage; the ubiquitous Ginsberg chanted mantras at dawn.

Having raised $4,200, Graham never looked back from that first Mime Troupe appeal. Indeed, he saw that the Troupe's politics could ultimately only get in the way of this new phenomenon taking place in San Francisco. A month later he went one better with a second appeal, holding it down in the city's predominantly black Fillmore section in the second-floor ballroom at 1805 Geary Street that would become inextricably linked with his name. To the local population the Fillmore Theater was San Francisco's very own Apollo, the venue where all the leading R&B and soul stars had played since 1952, but on December 10 it filled up with white kids in Haight regalia who'd come to hear the Great Society and the Mystery Trend.

The San Francisco Mime Troupe, who satirized America's "stupified, conscience-less society."

At the third and final appeal on January 14, 1966, the Society and the Trend played again but this time were joined by the Grateful Dead— "formerly the Warlocks," as Graham insisted they be billed on the posters. Bill Graham had a pretty shrewd idea of the career he would now be pursuing. The General Patton of the Bay Area rock scene—the guy who would actually *organize* these hapless longhairs—had arrived.

Meanwhile, across the Bay in Berkeley, folkies and students looked askance at the new scene in San Francisco. To many of them it looked simply too hedonistic and apolitical—too Pranksterish by half. After all, Berkeley was home to the Free Speech Movement, its world-famous university the new hub of early Sixties' campus activism. When student

Jack Weinberg was arrested on October 1, 1964, for selling political material on Telegraph Avenue, it ignited the new left, establishing radical politics as a vital medium for youth expression.

It was the final throwing-off of Fifties' repression in the era of civil rights, birth control, and anti-nuclear protest. U.C.-Berkeley president Clark Kerr dismissed the Free Speech movement as "a ritual of hackneyed complaints," but he was powerless to stop the rise of the fiery orator Mario Savio, who'd spent the summer in Mississippi and come home to find the university preventing students from collecting money for civil rights workers. Savio's famous speech in front of the university's administration building on December 2 was the birth of the sit-in: "There is a time when the operation of the machine becomes so odious, makes you so sick at heart, that you can't take part..." The mass arrest of eight hundred people that day was the largest in California's history.

Berkeley's finest. From left: Barry Melton, Joe McDonald, Bruce Barthol, John Francis Gunning, David Cohen.

On October 16, 1965, the day of the "Tribute to Doctor Strange" in San Francisco, a massive antiwar protest took place in Berkeley, with thousands marching from the campus to neighboring Oakland. As a portent of things to come, the Oakland chapter of the Hell's Angels decided to align themselves with the forces of repression by stomping the protestors' heads. Furthermore, their new chum Ken Kesey opted to sabotage the proceedings after being invited to speak by the Vietnam Day Committee. Rolling into town from La Honda in the bus, which had been adorned that day with military symbols, he made a sardonic speech to the crowd, accusing them of playing "*their* game," and then played a wheezy rendition of "Home On The Range" on a small harmonica. The yawning gulf between acid pranks and campus righteousness was becoming only too obvious.

Yet Berkeley itself was waking up to acid culture, most obviously in

the music of an electric band called Country Joe and the Fish. Joe McDonald had moved up to Berkeley from Los Angeles to be near the peacenik action, forming the Instant Action Jug Band not long after hitting town. Early in 1965 he met another émigré Angeleno, Barry Melton, on the Berkeley campus, and together they recorded the *Songs of Opposition* EP in the living room of Chris Strachwitz, owner of the Bay Area blues label Arhoolie. Folkies though they were, Melton opted to play electric guitar on "Superbird" and "I Feel Like I'm Fixin' To Die Rag," a pointer in the direction the Jug Band would take when reincarnated as Country Joe and the Fish. The EP, consisting of McDonald's songs on one side and two tracks by fellow folkie Peter Krug on the other, sold poorly but provided the springboard for the band's full electric sound.

The Family Dog
promote the
Avalon Ballroom.

Living in an apartment behind the Jabberwock folk club near the Berkeley campus, McDonald started dropping large amounts of acid and writing songs like "Bass Strings" and "Section 43," eventually recorded for a seminal EP in the summer of '66. Packing out the Jabberwock and the Cabale on San Pablo Avenue, the Fish quickly became Berkeley's local acid rock heroes. "There's a particular mix in Berkeley of politics, art and culture and music, and we hit it right on the nose," McDonald later reminisced. "We had the attitude people wanted to have. Like Woody Guthrie said,

'I WANT TO BE THE PERSON TO TELL YOU SOMETHING YOU ALREADY KNEW'"

73

L. S. D.*

MELLOW AND BLUE

WITH DIAMOND LOU

* LOU'S SWINGING DEN

RAE'S IN "B" TWEEN

1784 HAIGHT ST.

CLOSE COVER FOR SAFETY

ALLIED PRINTING
TRADES UNION LABEL COUNCIL
SAN JOSE, CALIF.

MONARCH MATCH CO. SAN JOSE, CAL.

Tripping the Switch

THE ACID TESTS WERE GETTING SERIOUS.
The second one, held in San José on December 4, 1965, was flooded with kids who'd spilled out of the Rolling Stones' show that night at the San José Civic Auditorium. Tom Wolfe called it "the first mass acid experience," and *Whole Earth Catalog* founder Stewart Brand noted that **THERE WAS A DISTINCT "WHIFF OF DANGER" IN THE AIR.** No less a personage than Owsley Stanley III showed up for the third Test at Muir Beach Lodge in Marin County on December 18. Ironically, "The Bear" had a bad trip–a hallucinogenic horror-show for which he ever after blamed Ken Kesey.

On January 8, 1966, the Acid Test finally came to San Francisco—to the Fillmore, to be precise. It was the city's first taste of the Pranksters' psychedelic bombardment—what Marshall McLuhan termed "sensory overload" and Haight historian Charles Perry called "an overpowering simultaneity." Paramount in the spectacle was a new kind of dancing, relaxed, trippy, flowing with the hypnotic groove of the music and the colors and shapes brought on by the acid. "The Tests were thousands of people, all hopelessly stoned, all finding themselves in a room full of other thousands of people, none of whom they were afraid of," said Jerry Garcia, whose band played the Fillmore that night. Rave culture starts here. In the Fillmore audience was Rock Scully of the Family Dog, who'd been unwise enough to schedule a dance that very same night at

75

the California Hall across town. (The Dogsters had run buses between the two venues in an effort not to lose too much of their audience.) Watching the Grateful Dead at the Test, Scully knew that this was the band he wanted to manage, not the Charlatans. They may have struck him as "the world's ugliest (and least hip) band," as he later reminisced, but they had something George Hunter's band would never have: They were *musically* in synch with the drug culture, not just stylistically. Not long after the Test, Scully sold his share of the Family Dog to Chet Helms.

The Fillmore Test, broken up by cops at 2:00 A.M. despite the fact that LSD was still perfectly legal, turned out to be merely a prelude to an altogether more ambitious happening dreamed up by *Whole Earth* visionary Stewart Brand and artist Ramon Sender, and staged at the Longshoremen's Hall on the weekend of January 20/21, 1966. The Trips Festival, as it was dubbed, was the culmination of the Tests and the Mime Troupe appeals—the ultimate Test, the Test gone truly public. Billed as "a new medium of communication and entertainment, a drugless PSYCHEDELIC EXPERIENCE," it brought together the many strands of the Bay Area revolution: Musicians, dancers, S.F. State students, Berkeley activists, Open Theater actors, Ron Boise and his Electric Thunder sculptures, and above all the Merry Pranksters, to whom Brand and colleagues offered the Saturday night as an Acid Test. "The general tone of things has moved from the self-conscious Happening to a more JUBILANT occasion where the audience PARTICIPATES because it's more fun to do so than not," the organizers wrote in their announcement. "Maybe this is the ROCK REVOLUTION." It was.

Come the Saturday night, the Pranksters were in their element: Ken Babbs ensconsed amidst a huge agglomeration of pipes and platforms in the center of the hall, supervising the many projectors and flashlight

The Trips Festival, January, 1966: "Maybe this is the ROCK REVOLUTION."

machines, Neal Cassady lurching around in a gorilla costume, the fugitive Kesey encased inside an enormous space helmet. Paul Krassner of *The Realist* described what he saw as "a ballroom surrealistically seething with a couple of thousand bodies stoned out of their everlovin' bruces in crazy costumes and obscene makeup." Also wandering around in the midst of the madness was a man who struck Bob Weir of the Dead—and almost everyone else—as "an asshole with a clipboard." It was Bill Graham, who'd been hired to maintain some semblance of order but who was feeling thoroughly freaked out by his first experience of the Pranksters at work.

"Bill didn't have a clue," remembered Owsley. "I realized he was half-terrified by what it was and was doing everything he could to control it and suppress his realization that there was something special going on here." To Graham's disbelief and everyone else's, the Trips Festival made a profit of $16,000: It turned out this hippie shit could actually *pay*. More to the point, it kicked off the brief golden age of San Francisco, before the tourists and the record companies swooped down on the place. In the words of Tom Wolfe, "the Haight-Ashbury era began that weekend."

Graham's discomfort at the Trips was symptomatic of his uneasy relationship with the Haight underground—a relationship that came to a head when he fell out that winter with Chet Helms and his partner John Carpenter. Graham and Helms had agreed to co-promote three shows, starting with "A Tribal Stomp," starring the Airplane and Big Brother and the Holding Company, on February 19, 1966, and climaxing in three galvanizing shows by the Butterfield Blues Band at the end of March. It soon became apparent, however, that Graham's approach to rock'n'roll conflicted markedly with Helms'. Graham was abrasive and abusive where Helms was seen to be one of the hippies.

Chet Helms, who opened the legendary Avalon Ballroom in April, 1966.

"Chet was in it because it was a religious experience," says David Rubinson, who'd worked with Bill Graham and even brought the Mime Troupe to New York. "It was something that was coming through him to the people, whereas Bill was a real refugee businessman. I was a tough Jewish boy from New York myself, so I knew Bill inside out: He was my uncle and my aunt and my brother-in-law." Chet Helms, says Paul Kantner, was "more in tune with what San Francisco was at that time—sybaritic, hedonistic, party-loving people. Chet didn't get up as early in the morning as Bill prided himself on doing, but the Family Dog in its own way was a better operation for the scene, and much more embracing."

"Getting up early in the morning:" This was always Graham's great cry, and it was at the core of the falling-out between him and Helms. The morning after the Butterfield band thrilled the Fillmore crowd with their proto-raga epic "East-West," Graham stole a march on Helms by jumping out of bed at dawn to call Butterfield's manager Albert Grossman in New York, thus ensuring that he bagged Butterfield's next San Francisco dates for himself. Helms couldn't forgive what he saw as a sly and underhanded way of doing business, so he and Carpenter found their own ballroom in the old Puckett Academy of Dance building on the corner of Sutter and Van Ness, renaming it the Avalon Ballroom. The venue opened for business on April 22, 1966, with a double bill consisting of the Blues Project and the Great Society.

For more than two years the Avalon and the Fillmore battled it out as the two leading rock ballrooms in San Francisco. They were the venues where the major Bay Area and out-of-town bands played, and they competed furiously, rewarding the loyalty of musicians, poster designers, and light show artists. If Graham was the eventual winner of the battle—because the Family Dog was undercapitalized,

The Dead at the Avalon, September, 1966. "Skull and Roses" poster by Kelly and Mouse.

according to Helms; because Helms let too many of his friends in, according to Graham—it is probably fair to say that the Avalon better embodied the spirit of the Haight than the Fillmore did. Helms' aesthetic was less rooted in Broadway showbiz, more attuned to the ecstatic, egoless collectivity that was beginning to define the "hippie" generation.

"In the early days, the audience and the bands were on the same plane," Big Brother's Sam Andrew remembered. "It's an understatement to say that the vibe at the shows was exuberant—it was *rhapsodic*. It felt like everyone was joined by this electric current, and they were all part of it." Significantly, where the Fillmore light shows would pick out the "stars" of the new bands, the visual artists at the Avalon rarely employed spotlights. In the words of Ed Sanders, whose band the Fugs played both venues, "it was good for the ego/to dissolve in the visual gestalt."

Tripping the light phantastic: "It was good for the ego to dissolve in the visual gestalt."

The techniques of the light shows had first been pioneered by S.F. State art professor Seymour Locks in the early Fifties, then introduced to the Beat scene by art student Elias Romero. By 1962 Romero was doing shows in conjunction with the Mime Troupe, influencing such stars of the psychedelic light show era as Bill Ham and Tony Martin. Ham was a painter and Family Dog compadre who would mix watercolor and oil paints and project them onto a screen above bands with an old army surplus machine he'd acquired. Like Martin, who worked primarily at the Avalon, he developed the art of synchronizing visuals with rhythms, creating pulsating globular effects that blew the minds of lysergic revellers. Other key light show artists included Ray Anderson and Ben Van Meter, both working toward the same ends.

Contemporaneous with the art of the light shows was the work of the poster artists hired to publicize the "dance concerts" at the Fillmore and

the Avalon. More than any other artifacts of the time these posters have come to define the look of the San Francisco scene in all its playful, swirling beauty. Again, significantly, the Avalon's posters tended to be more hieroglyphically extreme than the Fillmore's, with the shapes of letters expanding and distorting as though viewed on an acid trip. The era's first great poster—often referred to as "The Seed"—was the handbill for the Charlatans' summer residency at the Red Dog, hand-drawn by George Hunter and Mike Ferguson. Its antique Wild West style influenced many artists, including Wes Wilson, who became Bill Graham's main poster artist after the Trips Festival.

Light-show operators created pulsing globular effects that blew minds at the Fillmore and Avalon.

Chet Helms' first posters were the work of Family Dog member Alton Kelley, who'd moved to San Francisco from Connecticut in 1964 and who, in the summer of 1966, formed a highly successful partnership with Detroit-born Stanley Miller, a.k.a. "Mouse." (Their studio on Henry Street also provided a rehearsal room for Big Brother and the Holding Company.) Like Wilson, Kelley and Mouse revelled in taking classic American iconography—from vintage automobiles to Native Americans—and psychedelically customizing it. Among those who followed them into the acid kingdom were Victor Moscoso, Bob Fried, Lee Conklin, and Bill Graham's wife Bonnie (née MacLean). The most celebrated of all the artists who took "The Seed" as their source point was Rick Griffin, a Southern Californian surfer boy who'd seen the Charlatans at the Red Dog and passed the Acid Test in Watts. With his painting for the album cover of the Grateful Dead's *Aoxomoxoa* of 1968, the San Francisco artwork style reached its freaky peak.

By the spring of 1966, with the Fillmore and the Avalon open and concert posters routinely being torn from telegraph poles to be kept as psychedelic art, the Haight era was truly under way. "In early '66 the Haight was heaven for anybody with long hair," recalled Spencer

Dryden, who would replace Skip Spence in the Jefferson Airplane drum seat later that year. "About eight hundred dyed-in-the-wool hippies and that's it. It was a family thing. No tourists. Everybody *did* live together and *did* help each other out." Things may have been stirring in other American cities, but San Francisco was the golden hippietopia that mind-expanded adolescents across the nation were fantasizing about. Already kids were pouring into the Greyhound terminal on 7th Street in unheard-of numbers: In the first half of 1966 alone, 1,231 runaways were reported to be at large in San Francisco. Close to fifteen thousand "hippies" were estimated to be living in the Haight-Ashbury neighborhood.

The year had begun with the opening at 1535 Haight Street of the Psychedelic Shop, run by two brothers who'd grown up working as stock boys in a Woolworth's store managed by their father. Ron and Jay Thelin saw the Shop less as a store than as the center of a "Haight-Ashbury communications network"—a place to meet and post messages. Not long after, they became involved in the Haight's very own news sheet, the *Oracle,* brainchild of editor Allen Cohen and acid evangelist Michael Bowen. Around the same time, Dr. David Smith opened the Haight-Ashbury Free Clinic, whose principal duty lay in treating the neighborhood's many acid casualties. Boutiques like Mnasidika sold the hip threads that anyone with cashflow was wearing. Everywhere one looked there were becloaked kids emerging from the cocoon of adolescence, doused in patchouli oil and parading along the streets: Middle-class gypsies in moccasins, driving painted VW vans, united in outraging the status quo, flaunting their sexuality and their pharmacopoeia.

Manhattan may have had its East Village, and Los Angeles its Venice—may have had the same drugs and cockroaches and open-toed

The Haight at its height: "About 800 dyed-in-the-wool hippies and that's it. Everybody *did* live together and *did* help each other out."

sandals—but their scenes were a good deal more fragmented than San Francisco's, which really *was* villagelike in its intimacy and communality. Above all, there was an almost religious zeal about acid in the Haight. LSD was the path to a truer beauty, to the enlightenment and the apprehension of the divine glimpsed by ancient seers, leading away from what Nietzsche called the "benighted souls" who had "no idea how cadaverous and ghostly their 'sanity' appears as the intense throng of Dionysiac revelers sweeps past them." Something was happening, and Mr. Jones would *never* know what it was.

Above all, the sound of San Francisco had arrived—"intuitive and unpolished and rhapsodic and endless," in the words of Janis Joplin biographer Myra Friedman. The Airplane were playing regularly at the Fillmore and the Avalon; so, through the spring and early summer, were the Charlatans and the Great Society and the Quicksilver Messenger Service and Big Brother and the Holding Company. The Airplane headlined Bill Graham's three-night "Sounds of the Trips Festival" on the weekend of 4/6 February, and Ralph Gleason made them the focus of a major overview of the Bay Area scene, "San Francisco—The New Liverpool." Pretty soon the band was being courted by the record companies in New York and Los Angeles, still uncertain as to what they were dealing with or how in hell they would market it. Eventually they signed with RCA-Victor for the unprecedented advance of $25,000—not that they would initially see much of it, thanks to the artful dodgings of manager Matthew Katz. (When Marty Balin challenged him on the subject one day, Katz had the gall to inform the Airplane co-founder that he was fired from his own group. The band finally parted company with their would-be Svengali in June.)

Jefferson Airplane Takes Off, recorded in Hollywood in the spring, consisted mainly of Balin ballads shot through with Jorma Kaukonen's

The Haight as hippietopia: Kids swarm into "San Fransico."

89

post-folk-rock guitar licks and lifted by the voices of Balin and Signe Toly Anderson: It was, in the words of Paul Kantner, "a folk music album …electrified a *little* bit…" If "It's No Secret" was a blueprint for the charged, anthemic style the Airplane would make their own, and "Come Up The Years" a tremulous folk-rock ballad about an archetypal femal runaway on the scene, the rest of *Takes Off* was a tad two-dimensional—and certainly a long way off from the full flowering of acid rock.

The Grateful Dead, meanwhile, had gone south to Los Angeles, to live in a house on the outskirts of Watts with Owsley and his acid lab. The band was in Watts when the Merry Pranksters—*sans* Ken Kesey, who'd split for Mexico to avoid a charge of marijuana possession—blew through town and held an infamous Test there on February 12, dosing everyone (including some of the children) with heavily spiked Kool-Aid. Among their number now was Carolyn "Mountain Girl" Adams, then heavily pregnant by Kesey. At the Test she hit it off with Garcia, himself married with a newborn daughter: By the end of the year, the two of them would be an item. As it happens, things were starting to unravel in the Prankster camp, thanks mainly to Kesey's absence. Pro- and anti-Ken Babbs factions were forming among Kesey's original followers. Nor did a hysteria-fueling "exposé" of the Pranksters' acid antics in *Life*—by photo-essayist Larry Schiller, later famous (or infamous) for his coverage of the O.J. Simpson trial—exactly help matters.

"We were guinea-pigging more or less continuously, tripping frequently if not constantly," recalled Jerry Garcia of the Dead's stay in Watts. With Owsley and his partners Tim Scully and Melissa Cargill turning out tabs in awesome quantities, the band was expected to sample each new batch, as well as to adhere to a bizarre carnivorous diet that the Acid King insisted on. Only when Rock Scully came down

Outside the Psychedelic Shop, opened by the Thelin brothers in January, 1966.

from San Francisco to join them did they begin to get any work done, busying themselves with some of the material that would surface on their first album for Warner Brothers: An old Appalachian song called "Cold Rain And Snow," an old Gus Cannon jug song, "Viola Lee Blues," and a Garcia original, "Cream Puff War," that took oblique potshots at the soapbox radicals of Berkeley.

Slowly, from the many ingredients that went into the original Warlocks/Dead mix—from Stanley Brothers bluegrass to Sonny Boy Williamson via Lesh's immersion in serial and experimental music— the band was fashioning a new and spacey West Coast electric blues-rock, helped not a little by the state-of-the-art sound equipment that Owsley, an electronics buff, was buying for them.

By the time the Dead came home in April, they had honed their sound to the point where it could withstand being drawn out into long trippy jam sessions: Here was a bunch of musicians that genuinely communicated with each other onstage, regardless of how ripped they were. Being out of town, moreover, had only increased their mystique in the Haight, and Rock Scully was able to up their rate to $350 a show. Scully it was, too, who found the twenty-six-room ranch near Novato, north of the city, where the Dead would spend much of the summer— rehearsing, hanging out, and cavorting with naked teenage girls on acid. Verily this was "rock star heaven," as Jorma Kaukonen, a frequent visitor to the ranch, recalled.

Jerry Garcia and friends take a stroll down Haight Street.

If the Dead were "psychedelic Indians," wrote Charles Perry, then their friendly rivals the Quicksilver Messenger Service were "drugstore cowboys." Originally formed as a backing group for Dino Valente, an underground folk legend whose "Get Together" had been a staple of the hootenanny circuit, Quicksilver had had their plans scotched when Valente went to jail on a marijuana charge in the late fall of 1965.

Waiting for him to get out, they lived the lysergic life in a dank basement in North Beach. "These were the very early days of psychedelia," remembered lead guitarist John Cipollina. "Lots of LSD, no money, and lots of living off the street, which, coming from a good family, was very strange to me."

On his release, Valente was immediately busted again, so the band—Cipollina, singer Jimmy Murray, rythm guitarist/vocalist Gary Duncan, bassist/vocalist David Freiberg, and drummer Greg Elmore—opted to go it alone. By early '66 the QMS were living in a shack in Larkspur and being managed by one Ambrose Hollingsworth, who ran a school of psychic magic up in Petaluma. The shack instantly became a den of dexedrine ingestion and sexual iniquity, a sanctuary for runaway teen vixens like the girls who went on to marry Duncan and Freiberg. In spare moments they rehearsed Bo Diddley songs like "Mona" and "Who Do You Love," transforming them from choogling garage-band staples into the fully fledged acid jams they were playing at the Fillmore and the Avalon. By the summer a new manager, Ron Polte, had moved them even deeper into Marin County, to a ranch in Olema.

All the San Francisco bands were turning the rules of the pop music industry on their heads, blurring the distinction between artist and audience to the point where stardom became a dead issue. In the words of original *Rolling Stone* staffer Michael Lydon, "San Francisco's secret was not the dancing, the light shows, the posters, the long sets, or the complete lack of stage act, but the idea that all of them together were the creation and recreation of a community." For Bob Weir, the whole scene was like "a contact high." Even between the bands there was a camaraderie, a fellow feeling, that was completely new to pop culture. "It was a very encouraging scene," noted Paul Kantner. "At radio stations we'd take tapes of the Dead or Quicksilver or whoever we'd

The Dead outside Peggy Caserta's hippie boutique Mnasidika: Weir, Lesh, Pigpen, Garcia, Kreutzmann, and unidentified friend.

meet. There was a sense of 'We're all in this together.'"

Tied in with this sense of interconnectedness was the privileging of live performance over recording—of the evanescent, explosive event over the sterile and synthetic vinyl artifact. "The important thing about San Francisco rock'n'roll," said Ralph Gleason, "is that the bands here all sing and play live and not for recordings. You get a different sound at a dance: It's harder and more direct." Marty Balin told Richard Goldstein that the Beatles were "too complex to influence anyone around here— they're a studio sound;" Gary Duncan opined that "in the studio you attack things intellectually—onstage it's all emotion."

For outsiders, this suspicion of the recording process was simply the cover for a general sloppiness. "We looked pretty cynically at the West Coast rock scene," admitted John Sebastian of the Lovin' Spoonful. "Everybody was talking about all these psychedelic bands and we'd go and watch them rehearse and they were all loaded. I could never fathom how they even came up with the twelve tunes they needed for an album." On the other hand, the Jefferson Airplane reached a point when they said the Beach Boys would never work at the Fillmore—a point that tied in with a particularly vitriolic rivalry between San Francisco and Los Angeles.

Chet Helms called L.A. "plastic" and "uptight," while Joe McDonald described the place as "a short-sleeved velour pussycat with a plastic hard-on." In response, Frank Zappa claimed that San Franciscans had "a more rustic-than-thou approach" and that "everybody dressed up in 1890s garb, all pretty specific codified dress," partially echoing the words of Reyner Banham, the expatriate champion of L.A., who wrote that "prefabricated Yankee houses and prefabricated New England attitudes" had been "dumped unmodified" on the coast of northern California. At root this was a fruitless argument—one that would

Drugstore cowboys the Quicksilver Messenger Service. From left: Greg Elmore, Gary Duncan, John Cipollina, Jimmy Murray, David Freiberg.

culminate with the Monterey Pop Festival the following summer—about naturalness and authenticity versus hype and commerce.

The widening gap between the old-school recording business and San Francisco's new wave of live rock bands was illustrated perfectly when two of the scene's cutting-edge bands, the Charlatans and the Great Society, attempted to record for the Autumn label. Wearing his producer's hat, Sly Stone treated both acts like the dorky little Top 40 bands who auditioned for Tom Donahue at Mother's. The Charlatans cut four shambolic tracks from their Red Dog repertoire—"Jack Of Diamonds," "Baby Won't You Tell Me," "The Blues Ain't Nothin'," and "Number One"—but found it hard to work with a man as brusque and domineering as Sly.

The Great Society had a similar experience. Inspired by seeing the Airplane and formed in the fall of 1965 by drummer/film-maker Jerry Slick with his singer wife Grace and guitarist brother Darby, the group played a nightmarish audition for Donahue. "They threw Mother's open during the daytime in a cattle-call that was advertised in the media," recalled Darby Slick. "Sly was there as A&R and we played 'Father Bruce' and a couple of other tunes. Most of the other bands were Top 40, and they were laughing at us."

Supposedly "Big Daddy" Donahue was highly smitten by the comely Mrs. Slick, which was why the Great Society was given a recording contract, but it made little difference when it came time to enter the studio. "Sly tried," said Darby Slick. "He wanted us to run rehearsals more efficiently, but we just kept handing him joints…he probably reported back to Donahue, 'I can't do anything with these guys.'" Out of these sessions came the group's first Autumn single, Darby's modal novelty song "Free Advice," and the original, endearingly primitive version of Grace's timeless "Somebody To Love"—supposedly the

The Great Society. From left: Darby Slick, Jerry Slick, David Miner, Bard Dupont, Grace Slick.

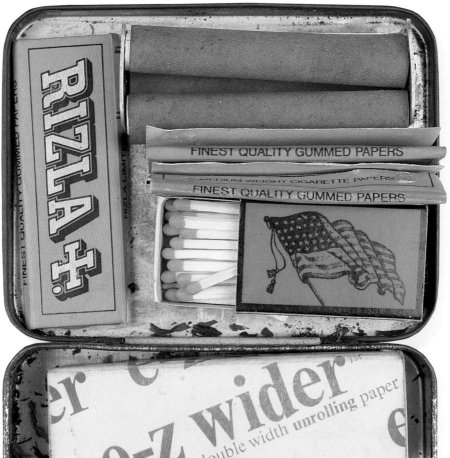

fiftieth take Sly put them through. The band soon felt at odds with the Top 40-oriented Autumn roster—in the words of Gene Sculatti, "worlds were colliding" here. Drummer Jan Errico, who'd left the Vejtables to join the Mojo Men (despite being a woman), put it still more succinctly:

"What separated the groups was simple: Who was doing drugs and who wasn't."

Roll another number for the road: Assorted paraphernalia for the modern pothead.

The Great Society were definitely doing drugs.

Autumn was falling apart, in any case: Big Daddy was dropping acid and Mighty Mitch dying of Hodgkin's Disease. "You know," Donahue remembered, "you're taking acid three or four times a week and it's very hard to talk to thirty-seven distributors and ask them the first day where your money is, the second day what they're doing about your records and the third day where your money is." One afternoon in April, 1966, Jan Errico came by Donahue's office on Dorman Avenue and found the door padlocked.

Autumn was over.

CHAPTER 2
ORANGE SUNSHINE

Graduation
DAY

"Summer of '66 is when the Sixties started rolling. Up until now it was all Pop, but suddenly up and down the coast it is one big endless party. Something is happening, something is growing out there."

ROCK SCULLY, *Living with the Dead*

IN MARCH,1966, there were race riots on the streets of Los Angeles: Further riots would follow in Chicago, Cleveland, and Brooklyn. IN APRIL, *TIME* MAGAZINE DECLARED "SWINGING LONDON" THE CAPITAL CITY OF THE WORLD, AND PREDICTED THAT A MILLION DOSES OF LSD WOULD BE CONSUMED THAT YEAR. THE BEATLES, spearheading the new sound of rock, were having a grueling time on tour in the States following the

much-publicized interview in which John Lennon's ill-chosen words described the band as "more popular than Jesus now." The group's August 29 appearance at San Francisco's Candlestick Park would be their last ever in America.

The San Francisco that Janis Joplin found when Chet Helms persuaded her to come back from Texas at the beginning of June 1966 was a very different place from the city she had fled, burned out and skeletal from speed, in the spring of 1965. She said of her Avalon Ballroom debut as the new lead singer of Big Brother and the Holding Company that "it was the most thrilling time in my life...I mean, I had never seen a hippie dance before, man, and then I was up there in the middle of one."

Fortunately, in that summer of 1966, Joplin was in considerably better shape than she'd been the year before. She was also singing better than ever—in a bluesier, more Bessie Smith-esque vein than Helms was used to. Austin's own psychedelic stars, the 13th Floor Elevators, had liked her raucous, caterwauling sound so much they'd asked her to join the band as co-lead singer with Roky Erickson. Rivers made it to Austin just in time to bag her for Big Brother.

Helms had taken note of Signe Anderson in the Jefferson Airplane and Grace Slick in the Great Society, and he figured a "chick singer" was just what the Holding Company needed to become something more than a rather leaden psychedelic blues band. Initial rehearsals at the Kelley-Mouse studios were not promising, however: The band was unsure about this unprepossessing Southern girl who chugged bourbon and came on to every male in sight.

An English girl who'd been in the Haight recalls:

Janis knew exactly what it meant to be a gutsy, ballsy girl, to want to do

Janis Joplin and friend in the Haight: "She was a plain girl who wanted deep down to be thought of as pretty."

105

everything the boys did, and then to suffer because she was not
feminine enough. She knew all about those pent-up feelings that you
can only get out in the big scream, about the claustrophobia that comes
from a straight upbringing and background…She was a plain girl who
wanted to be loved as a girl, who wanted deep down to be thought of as
pretty. No man, she would say, could ever give her what she sang
about…

Joplin picked up the vibes from the band and muttered threats about
going back to Port Arthur. But when the group moved out to an old
hunting lodge near Lagunitas in the West Marlin hills, things began to
gel. By the late summer, Big Brother even had a recording deal—a
laughably exploitative contract with R&B veteran Bobby Shad's
Mainstream label in Chicago. "simply because we hadn't really put in a
lot of time in clubs. I was the only one who'd played in a rock'n'roll band
before that." (Barry Melton of Country Joe and the Fish called James
Gurley "the founder of psychedelic guitar…the first man in space.")

In the lodge, Joplin bonded with James Gurley's wife Nancy, whose
exotic hippie dress sense—lots of lace and velvet, and masses of
jewelry—she quickly began to emulate. At night she would hang out in
the local bars shooting pool or boozing with her new pal "Pigpen"
McKernan of the Grateful Dead, who were now in residence down the
road in Camp Lagunitas. Janis and Pigpen were the two great
unreconstructed drinkers of the San Francisco scene, the blues nuts
who didn't give a damn that people now considered alcohol to be
horribly uncool. Both of them would always be fundamentally out of
place in the Haight scene.

The Dead themselves were in the process of moving into a large
Victorian mansion at 710 Ashbury Street, transforming the house into a

Big Brother's little
soul sister: "She
knew all about those
pent-up feelings you
can only get out in
the big scream…"

prototype rock commune. By October the place would be legendary: In the early evening you'd find members of the band and their entourage sprawled across the porch, chewing the breeze and waiting for the fog to roll in off the ocean. Pigpen had staked out a lair behind the kitchen, and Neal Cassady could often be found in the attic. The house also served as the offices of the Haight-Ashbury Legal Organization, or HALO. The band was working conscientiously on its music, cutting demos at the Commercial recorders studio with an engineer friend of the Quicksilver Messenger Service, Dan Healy.

Toward the end of the year, Tom Donahue—then in the process of selling the Autumn catalog to Warner Bros—recommended that Warner's Vice President Joe Smith come up to San Francisco to check out some of the bands, particularly the Dead. Smith was general manager of the Warner Brothers label, and one of the few L.A. executives to go up to the Bay Area. He claimed that Donahue told him, "I can deliver every other band up there for $25,000 apiece"—so much for Big Daddy's hippie principles. When Smith did venture up to the Bay Area to see the Dead, he thought the Bacchanalian ballroom scene was like "Fellini on stage," but he was sufficiently intrigued to discuss a contract with Rock Scully. The band made it a central condition of any deal that Smith drop acid with them. He declined but they signed anyway—a contract negotiated by rising rock lawyer Brian Rohan that would give the Dead unprecedented control over their recordings.

David Simpson, a Haight-Ashbury community leader, said:

It is very important to know how closely the alternative community of San Francisco identified with the music of specific musicians—the Grateful Dead, the Jefferson Airplane, the Messenger Service, and Big Brother and the Holding Company. They were our bands, they were our

The Dead on Ashbury Street, "chewing the breeze and waiting for the fog to roll in off the ocean..." Clockwise from left: Lesh, Kreutzmann, Pigpen, Weir, Garcia.

musicians. Neither they nor we felt the distinction between the artists and the people, and it gave the music great strength. By 1968 nobody danced at rock concerts any more, but in 1966 and 1967 nobody sat down. It was quite impossible. The concerts were a melee of bodies. It was a wonderful inspired sense of oneness.

For Chet Helms, the scene was "mostly an organization of peers, people on an equivalent level. The Grateful Dead were accessible. For example, Jerry Garcia would lean off a two-foot stage and say [to a member of the audience], 'Hey, Pete, how's the old lady and the kids? Haven't seen you in a month of Sundays.'"

The first San Francisco band to sign with a major label, the Jefferson Airplane, was undergoing a period of major turmoil at this point. For starters, Skip Spence had started to go off the deep end with acid: After taking off for Mexico in the summer, he returned to California to find that Marty Balin had replaced him with Spencer Dryden, an experienced drummer from L.A. Now there were misgivings, too, about Signe Anderson—or rather, a desire on the part of Paul Kantner and Jack Casady to replace her with Grace Slick of the Great Society. Both men had watched Slick perform several times with the Society and felt that she would be a more appropriate frontperson for the Airplane than the wholesome Anderson.

The Great Society was in pretty rickety shape, in any case. Jerry and Grace Slick's marriage was coming apart at the seams, and Darby Slick was deep into smack. After a benefit show featuring both bands at the Fillmore on September 11, 1966, Jack Casady approached Grace backstage and asked her if she would consider joining the Airplane. When she told her husband of the offer, he advised her to accept. Airplane manager Bill Thompson bought her contract for $750, "probably

Inside 710 Ashbury, hippie pad to end all hippie pads.

the greatest move since whoever bought Manhattan from the Indians." Airplane fans were upset by the departure of Signe Anderson, who was undeniably the better singer, but soon took to Slick's feisty punk-princess hauteur. "She was extraordinary, as we all knew she'd be," said Paul Kantner. "We got somebody who was really one of the boys and committed her to the cause." At the end of October, the band flew to Los Angeles to begin work on Surrealistic Pillow.

The band for whom nothing seemed to go right was the Charlatans. After having a miserable experience in the studio with Sly Stone, they were recommended to Lovin' Spoonful producer Erik Jacobsen by their Family Dog friend Luria Castell. Jacobsen, smitten with their Barbary Coast image—bowler hats and straw boaters, bootlace ties and walking canes—signed them to a laugable deal with Kama Sutra, a self-consciously "psychedelic" New York label which was already the Spoonful. When the band started work on an album at Coast Recorders, It rapidly became clear that things weren't going to work out with Jacobsen. "He thought he'd heard something in us," Mike Wilhelm told Alec Palao, "but when he got us in the studio he didn't hear it anymore. To this day I don't know what he was looking for." Jacobsen's desire to disengage himself from the project may have had more to do with the fact that the band dosed him with DMT amidst the Victorian gewgaws piled up in George Hunter's pad.

Whatever the truth, Kama Sutra balked when they heard the Charlatans' version of Buffy Sainte-Marie's "Codine"—intended as their first single—and they positively *freaked* when they saw George Hunter's proposed ad for the record, drawn in the style of "The Seed" and boasting the catchy slogan, "Remedy for a Drugged Market." Instead, in October, 1966, they released a lame cover of an obscure Coasters' single, "The Shadow Knows," sung by Mike Ferguson and

Previous pages: (Left) Grace Slick boards the Airplane. From left: Kantner, Slick, Balin (in mirror,) Casady (seated,) Dryden, Kaukonen.

(Right) Slick flips the middle digit.

accorded the bare minimum of promotion. It stiffed. "We were the big deal at the Avalon and these other bands started eclipsing us," recalled Richie Olsen. "People like the Airplane had the deals, they had a plan and were managed and had the approach down. We were doing it all on our own, we didn't have any help." The truth was that the Charlatans now sounded almost quaint next to the Dead and the Airplane: As Dan Hicks put it, "the San Francisco sound, that meandering psychedelic guitar stuff, we didn't ever have that."

Erik Jacobsen would fare better with a band called Sopwith Camel. Formed by Peter Kraemer and Terry MacNeil in the spring of 1966, with Rod Albin originally featured on bass, the Camel had the biggest San Francisco pop hit yet with the winsome "Hello Hello" in January '67. Hip they would never be, however, despite a fine first album that included the classic "Frantic Desolation." When the Grateful Dead supported them at the Longshoreman's Hall in April 1967, their set went on for so long that the power was switched off halfway through Sopwith Camel's first song. No one seemed to care. Meanwhile, the Lovin' Spoonful, Jacobsen's earlier success story, blew any credibility they'd had in San Francisco when Steve Boone and Zal Yanovsky were busted with pot and then, supposedly, "cooperated" with the police by finking on the friend who'd sold to them. Cyril Jordan of the Flamin' Groovies maintained that the friend in question asked Bill Graham to blacklist them. "It was the first time you saw how much power the underground had," says Jordan. "All the hippies that smoked dope and thought the Spoonful were great dudes immediately turned on them and said, 'Fuck these assholes.' And that was the end of them."

On October 6, 1966, after a summer of hysteria about kids on acid jumping off rooftops, possession of LSD finally became illegal. The change in the law was commemorated by a "Love Pageant Rally" organized by

Overleaf: (Left) Hunter and Hicks, Barbary Coast dandies.

(Right) The amazing Charlatans. From left: Hunter, Olsen, Wilhelm, Dan Hicks, Ferguson.

115

Allen Cohen and Michael Bowen of the *San Francisco Oracle*. The rally was a celebration of innocence intended, in the words of the official invitation, to "overcome the paranoia and separation with which the State wishes to divide and silence the increasing revolutionary sense of Californians." To show their support for the event, the Grateful Dead and Big Brother and the Holding Company played for free in the Panhandle, the thin strip of parkland that paralleled Haight Street all the way to Golden Gate Park.

After it was over, a discussion between Cohen, Bowen, and Richard Alpert led to the idea of a "Human Be-In"—a "gathering of the tribes" that would serve as an umbrella for the different factions that made up the hippie revolution. It bothered the three of them that Haight-Ashbury was still regarded with scorn by the radicals of Berkeley, who decreed that political activism was incompatible with the passivity of "dropping out." "Berkeley distrusted rock'n'roll," noted Haight historian Charles Perry. "Throughout the McCarthy years rock had been the enemy and folk was the true revolutionary music...most of all, the politicos despised the Haight's lack of politics and resented the fact that these nobodies...had stolen their thunder as young rebels."

In a sense, Jerry Rubin and company were right: There was a political apathy about the hippies: As Tom Wolfe noted, "the political thing, the whole New Left, is all of a sudden like OVER on the hip circuit around San Francisco..." But what was really passé was the earnest self righteousness of the civil rights years. Ralph J. Gleason argued that "the Square Left" misunderstood the new rock culture: For him, what was happening in the Haight was "political acts of a different kind, a kind that results in Hell's Angels being the guardians of lost children..."

Foremost among the exponents of these "political acts of a different kind" were the Diggers, who formed in October after a meeting of the so-called "Artist Liberation Front," attended by, among others, Michael Bowen, Allen Ginsberg, the Thelin brothers, and novelist Richard Brautigan. Prime mover in this radical street troupe was Emmett Grogan, a charismatic anarchist who'd grown up on the Lower East Side of New York and whose bellicose rejection of liberal humanism drew heavily on the anti-institutional tactics of "systematic irrationality" practiced by Kesey and the Pranksters. With the help of fellow New Yorker Billy Murcott, Grogan wrote a series of aggressively cynical broadsides that held almost nothing sacred and even attacked what it perceived to be the empty psychedelic rituals of the Haight. "How long will you tolerate people transforming your trip into cash?" read one Digger leaflet. "Your style is being sold back to you..."

The Diggers' most radical initiative was to distribute free food in the Panhandle every afternoon, a response to the swelling ranks of homeless and impoverished teenagers flooding the Haight. They would scour market stalls and supermarket bins every day for discarded food, turning their spoils into soup. Many store-owners accepted the Diggers as the unofficial conscience of the streets—as "worker-priests"—but one butcher whacked Grogan with the flat side of a meat cleaver when the abrasive New Yorker called him "a fascist pig and a coward" for refusing to donate food.

Among the other events the Diggers organized was a "Rebirth of the Haight/Death of Money, Now" march down Haight Street, when assorted heads, Hell's Angels, children, and animals paraded down the main hippie thoroughfare protesting the culture of crass commercialism. Diggers wearing enormous animal masks designed by sculptor La Mortadella bore a coffin along the street representing the expiration of the filthy lucre, and runaway child Phyllis Willner stood aloft on the back of Hairy Henry Kot's Harley screaming "Freeeeeeee!"—a misdemeanor

Remedy for a Drugged Market.

CODINE

Insist on the Genuine Article

Keep in a Cool Place

Composed by Buffy St. Marie

Produced by Erik Jacobsen

32 BLUES 20

THE CHARLATANs

SWEET RELIABLE Productions

KAMASUTRA

Dist. by M.G.M.

that got Hairy Henry arrested along with his Angel brother Chocolate George. The arrests merely led to a further march, this time on Park Police Station, led by Michael McClure, Richard Brautigan, and another Angel celebrity, Freewheelin' Frank. Bail was raised and Henry and George were released.

The Pranksters themselves were drawing to the end of their golden period in the Bay Area, almost assuming the status of *éminences grises*. Having had an incalculable influence on everyone from the Dead to the Family Dog to the Diggers, spearheading the use of acid by the post-Beat generation, they were close to exhausted by their activities. But one last major Prankster event had been planned for Halloween: An "Acid Test Graduation," no less, to be held in a former ice-skating rink at the corner of Post and Steiner called Winterland. The poster for the event even boasted the fugitive Ken Kesey among its attractions, along with Neal Cassady and the Grateful Dead. Kesey, it transpired, had sneaked back into the U.S. from Mexico and had even talked to *San Francisco Chronicle* reporter Donovan Bess. The Graduation, he said, would be about "going beyond acid."

What Kesey didn't know was that the new entrepreneurs of the ballroom scene no longer wished to play along with the Captain and his pranks: Even Chet Helms felt that there was now "a very military tone to Kesey's trips." Indeed, Tom Wolfe claimed in *The Electric Kool-Aid Acid Test* that it was Helms who advised his arch-rival Bill Graham, who was promoting the "Graduation," to pull the plug on the event. All of a sudden, the scene had become mistrustful of Kesey, and of what precisely he meant by "going beyond acid." Graham himself saw Kesey as a psychedelic Elmer Gantry: Even the Dead began to distance themselves from him. "They won't change because they have too much money involved," Kesey muttered to Tom Wolfe as he scrambled to

George Hunter's ad for "Codine." It failed to amuse the bigwigs at MGM.

121

(FX 2) SAN FRANCISCO,OCT.6-(AP)-A large group of hippies greet the sunrise from a San Francisco hilltop on Friday beginning a three-day wake for the death of the hippie movement in the Haignt-Asnbury district.Summer hippies have been pouring out of town.More are expected go as San Francisco's chilly fall sets in.It is not the climate for bare feet and sleeping in the park,a policeman said,and we could use some bad weather to speed them on their way.(AP Wirephoto)1967

recover from this blow; "it was too big and too hot and they all got frightened." Hippies, it transpired, wanted something altogether more peaceful and Zenlike than anything Kesey envisaged; they were no longer prepared to go the distance with the Pranksters. There was something Learlike about the betrayal, as though the Haight were punishing its own spiritual godfather.

In the end, the Graduation was held in the much smaller Calliope Company Warehouse, with music by the Anonymous Artists of America. "I believe that our concept is changing," Kesey addressed the Halloween revellers. "It's been happening here in San Francisco. I believe there's a whole new generation of kids. They walk different…I can hear it in the music…For a year we've been in the garden of Eden. Acid opened the door to it." There was a slight sense of desperation about his words, and a distinct pathos set in as the crowd began to drift away, leaving Kesey with the inner Prankster circle—the faithful who gathered about him as dawn broke outside. On the stage, Neal Cassady wore a mortarboard and handed out diplomas.

"The most important thing was that it was time not to do the Tests anymore," said Ken Babbs afterwards. "It was time to move on. So we all moved up to Oregon." Kesey would end up serving ninety days in prison, and then five months on a work farm. A year after the Graduation he was back in Springfield, Oregon, with his wife and children. The other Pranksters scattered to various communes in California and New Mexico. Some became members of Wavy Gravy's Hog Farm down in L.A. (Wavy Gravy, formerly known as Hugh Romney, was an improvizational performer whose therapeutic work with autistic children met with some success. So did the Hog Farm, which ultimately became a huge organization, dealing with everything from performance art to light shows nationwide.) Neal Cassady washed up in Mexico,

where in early February, 1968 he was found by the side of a railway line, dead of a Seconal overdose. He was forty-two years old.

In the Haight, people tried to justify their betrayal of Kesey—the rejection of what Wolfe called "the troublesome…souped-up thing the Pranksters had always been into…" The real truth was that Bill Graham's San Francisco had won out over Ken Kesey's, and a more efficient marketing of Flower Power would now replace the outrageous chaos of the Acid Tests. Graham had consolidated his operation in the summer, working hard on his relationships with local merchants and finally obtaining the permit for the Fillmore that he had been denied for six months.

John Cipollina and Jimmy Murray of Quicksilver at the Human Be-In. Seated at right: A blissed-out Timothy Leary.

"What did Bill Graham bring to San Francisco?" asked David Rubinson of Columbia Records. "He brought delivery on promises… and it was all in cash. It was the most remarkable blending together of the Catskill Mountains aggressive mentality…and the people who were totally stoned." Pete Townshend of the Who felt that "without Bill, all these airheads would fall to bits." Even Mime Troupe/Digger activist Peter Cohon—now Peter Coyote, a famous actor whose voice can be heard promoting Isuzu cars on American television—conceded that "we always needed a Bill Graham or whatever to help us run these theater pieces…if he'd looked like Sonny Bono, I might really have pissed all over him, but he was always this *guy,* this guy who walked out of Auschwitz. So what the fuck did he care about shoulder-length hair?"

What should not be overlooked in any appraisal of Bill Graham, however, is just how much he did care about the music. "He was extremely soulful," says David Rubinson. "People paint him with one color, but my experience was very far from that." A particular point of pride with Graham was the way he mixed up different acts at the

Fillmore: He was almost pedagogic in his desire to educate hippies about black and Latin American music. It was not unusual to find Lightnin' Hopkins on a bill with the Jefferson Airplane or Junior Wells on a bill with the Grateful Dead. For Bill, Otis Redding's Fillmore show on December 20, 1966 was "the best gig I ever put on in my entire life."

Early in 1967, Graham began helping Bill Thompson to manage the Jefferson Airplane. Horrible fights ensued almost immediately between the promoter and the band. One evening, after Graham had suggested that they act a little more animated on stage, Paul Kantner sneered, **"Fuck that, that's show business."** Graham turned to him, paused, and shouted, **"SCHMUCK! What business do you think you're in?!"**

"What did Bill Graham bring to San Francisco? He brought delivery on promises...and it was all in cash."

Make Sure to Wear Some Flowers in Your Hair

NINETEEN SIXTY-SEVEN WAS A YEAR OF GREAT LANDMARKS in the worlds of rock and hippiedom. In San Francisco, it began with a magical congregation in the Polo Grounds of Golden Gate Park. The "Human Be-In," the so-called "gathering of the tribes," had been conceived by the editors of the *San Francisco Oracle* as a way of uniting the myriad entities which comprised the hippie underground. "Berkeley political activists and the love generation of Haight-Ashbury," announced the press release, "will join together with members of the new nation who will be coming from every state in the nation, every tribe of the young…TO POW-WOW, CELEBRATE, AND PROPHESY THE EPOCH OF LIBERATION, LOVE, PEACE, COMPASSION, AND UNITY OF MANKIND." Grateful Dead manager Rock Scully noted that "we have invited the Berkeley rads because we consider them outlaws like ourselves, but we make it a condition of their participating that there be **ABSOLUTELY NO RABBLE-ROUSING.**"

Advertised by a Rick Griffin poster that featured psychedelic Western lettering and a guitar-toting Native American warrior on a horse, the "pow-wow" promised a lineup of Frisco bands and campus firebrands, of Beat legends and psychedelic gurus. Indeed, one could almost argue that the event had been commandeered by a group of

aging bohemians (Ginsberg, Leary, Ferlinghetti, Snyder, Rubin, et. al.) who wanted to ensure they obtained an "in" with the new generation—especially since Leary, for one, was regarded by denizens of the Haight with suspicion. But it would be churlish to argue thus, considering how genuinely united the twenty thousand-odd people traipsing through Golden Gate Park on that golden winter morning of January 14 felt.

For Ginsberg, the Be-In was like Blake's vision of Eden: A shimmering sea of smiling faces, many belonging to people flying high on Owsley's new "White Lightning" acid. MC'd by Buddha, a Haight scenester and crony of Big Brother, the gathering was a peak moment of Utopian hippie bliss. "A lot of stoned people were wandering around blowing their minds on how many others were there," wrote Charles Perry. "It was like awakening to find you'd been reborn and this was your new family." Perry called it "one of the grand mythic events of the Haight mystique...the notion of a meeting without any purpose other than to be," and Steve Levine of the *Oracle* wrote that it was "a calm and peaceful approbation, a reaffirmation of the life spirit, a settling of the waters." In the midst of it all sat Timothy Leary, grinning helplessly in white cotton with petals tucked behind his ear.

Love Burgers on the Haight: The Dead play for free in the Panhandle.

Among the Berkeley contingent at the Be-In, significantly, were Country Joe and the Fish, the band whose music itself bridged the gulf between the hippies and the radicals. Back in June '66 the Fish had recorded an eponymous three-track EP that ranks among the first true psychedelic recordings to come out of the Bay Area. "Thing Called Love" was generic garage blues-rock, but "Bass Strings" and "Section 43" were trippy, eerily mesmerizing. "Got so high this time that you know/I'll never come down," Joe McDonald sang in his softest, spaciest voice on "Bass Strings." The instrumental "Section 43" was inspired by "The Hall of the Mountain King" in Peer Gynt, but the mesh of Barry Melton's rippling guitar runs and David Cohen's haunting organ pads created a druggy, almost Eastern quality. "No one had ever heard something like 'Section 43' or 'Bass Strings' before," McDonald said later. "At the moment of that EP we were the only people in the world doing that, an aspect of us that hasn't really been acknowledged." After the EP, even the formerly scathing *Berkeley Barb* began to rally to the Haight cause of rock and drugs and free love.

When the Fish set to work on their first Vanguard album their approach was similarly low on politics, high on acid poetics. Released in April '67, *Electric Music for the Mind and Body* was a psychedelic masterwork, a freaky lysergic journey featuring reworked versions of all three EP tracks, along with the exquisite "Porpoise Mouth," the chilling "Death Sound," and a hymn to the lead singer of the Jefferson Airplane called "Grace." "I think *Electric Music* is the best psychedelic record ever made," says McDonald modestly. "Millions of people have tripped to that album. It's guaranteed!"

McDonald completed his "crossing" from Berkeley to the Haight when he commenced an affair with the new princess of the San Francisco underground—or "the first hippie pinup girl," as Janis Joplin had now been dubbed. Not long after Big Brother and the Holding Company manager Julius Karpen moved the band back to the city from Lagunitas early in 1967, Janis began living with McDonald in a small apartment on Lyon Street. The relationship was fated to peter out—he liked acid, she preferred Southern Comfort—but for the time it was a notable celebrity coupling.

With Big Brother now established as a regular fixture at the

Avalon, Joplin was transforming herself into rock royalty. Swathed in silk and velvet, bedecked in bangles and feather boas, she wasn't interested in San Francisco anonymity. She wanted to be a star in the way that Mick Jagger was a star. She had also found her very own showstopper in the form of Willie Mae "Big Mama" Thornton's harrowing "Ball and Chain." Catching Thornton singing one night in a little joint on Divisadero Street, she went backstage to ask if she could use the song, which was perfect material for the persona of the tragic, hard-bitten blues mama Joplin was so keen to cultivate. Big Mama said she was welcome to it.

Other leading San Francisco bands were busy in the studio. Both the Grateful Dead and the Jefferson Airplane were cutting albums at RCA-Victor in Los Angeles: The Dead their first and the Airplane their second, both with producer Dave Hassinger. Recorded in three days on a speed marathon, *The Grateful Dead* was an unsatisfying compromise between the group's glorified-bar-band origins and their desire for free-flowing experimentation, produced by a man who was irredeemably square, in an unsympathetic Hollywood environment of velour and Naugahyde. Still, you could hear the Dead's sheer exuberance in the opening "The Golden Road (To Unlimited Devotion)," the first single, and in the versions of "Viola Lee Blues" and "Sitting On Top Of The World." "In the land of the dark," trumpeted the ad in the *Oracle,* "the ship of the sun is piloted by the Grateful Dead."

The Airplane's *Surrealistic Pillow* was a much more confident album, boasting two Top 10 singles in the revamped Great Society songs "Somebody to Love" and "White Rabbit." Ironically, Jerry Garcia was credited on the record as "musical and spiritual advisor": He had sat in on the sessions at the Victor studios, and his input on

Overleaf: Big Daddy Donahue and the staff of underground station KMPX, October '67.

the album's arrangements (and its title, come to that) was deemed by all concerned to have made the crucial difference to its success. "Embryonic Journey" was a solo instrumental derived from a piece Jorma Kaukonen had performed at clubs during his early folk days, while "White Rabbit" was based musically on Ravel's *Bolero* and lyrically on Lewis Carroll. "Adults were ragging at us for taking drugs," she said. "What I wrote the song for was to say, 'Why did you read me this stuff? Look at what this stuff *says*!' " A mixture of anthemic acid rock and haunting folk-pop ballads, *Pillow* was a considerable advance on *Takes Off*. Released with much accompanying fanfare in March 1967, it climbed as high as No. 3 on the album chart and confirmed the Airplane's status as the preeminent San Francisco band. For Slick, in particular, it was a triumph: Balin was a good singer, but Slick's strident tone was the band's new hallmark.

The "love generation" of Haight-Ashbury—celebrating love, peace, compassion, and the unity of mankind.

Along with the first-wave Bay Area bands—Quicksilver had also moved back to town early in the year—new groups were starting to make their presence felt on the scene. "The competition was fierce," recalled Richie Olsen of the Charlatans. "It was like, 'There's gold in them thar hills.' You had Steve Miller coming from Texas and the Youngbloods from New York, becoming 'San Francisco bands,' and we were going, 'Who *are* these people?!'"

The most promising by far was the five-piece Moby Grape, a band assembled by ex-Airplane manager Matthew Katz and featuring ex-Airplane drummer Skip Spence, whose song "My Best Friend" was included on *Surrealistic Pillow*. Katz had heard Peter Lewis singing at a club in L.A. and hooked him up with bassist Bob Mosley, bringing the pair north to San Francisco in the summer of 1966. From the Pacific Northwest came Jerry Miller (guitar) and Don Stevenson

(drums); Spence came into the picture when Lewis met him in Katz's office in August.

Cherry-picking band members doesn't usually work in pop music, but in Moby Grape's case it did. Great songs like "Fall on You" and "Changes" came tumbling out of the quintet, and electrifying shows were soon being played at venues like the Ark in Sausalito. When Columbia Records staff producer David Rubinson caught an Ark show at which Moby Grape were supporting the (pre-Steppenwolf) Sparrow, he watched them blow the headliners off the stage: "They came out and did forty-five minutes of the tightest, most musical, high-intensity stuff I'd ever heard—I couldn't believe what I was hearing."

With the word spread by peers like Neil Young and Steve Stills of the Buffalo Springfield, gigs followed at the Avalon and the Fillmore. Elektra's Paul Rothchild cut some demos with the band, and Atlantic expressed interest. In the end it was Rubinson, in February, 1967, who bagged their signatures for Columbia and took them down to L.A. to record their first album: "It took me a good six months to sign them, because everyone wanted them. Jac Holzman at Elektra, in fact, called me into a quiet meeting and offered me a job, provided I brought Moby Grape to the label."

With hindsight, Rubinson admitted he'd rushed Moby Grape through the sessions in March and April, but the resulting record is regarded today as a stone classic: A sizzling mix of San Francisco and Los Angeles, of the Dead and the Airplane and the Byrds and the Springfield, described beautifully by David Fricke as "an effervescent synthesis of choirboy folk-rock singing, clattering garage-rock propulsion and white R&B moxie." Lewis' Byrdsy influence was balanced out by the soulful intensity of Mosley, a Nordic-looking Bobby Bland wannabe, while Spence brought a whole other

Texan blues whizkid Steve Miller: "I knew I couldn't miss in San Francisco. The Dead and the Airplane barely knew how to tune their instruments."

sensibility to the table with songs like "Omaha" and "Indifference." "Skippy was always high on this other level," Lewis told Fricke, "yet he was an inspiration, always able to get people going on his trip, the most unique songwriter I ever met, imbued with the demonic, an *idiot savant.*"

Unfortunately, as Fricke noted in his sleevenote to the two-CD *Vintage: The Very Best of Moby Grape*, the band was "an object lesson in how not to succeed in the music business." The grotesque overselling of Moby Grape not only took in purple velvet press kits and an Avalon showcase to which writers were flown from all over America, but led to Columbia simultaneously releasing no fewer than five singles from the album—none of which, as a result, received any significant airplay. To top it all off, the night of the Avalon show Spence, Lewis, and Miller were busted in Marin County with three naked teenage girls. "We were the next big thing," Lewis reminisced, "but we didn't know what we had till we were through with that first album...we didn't have enough [hanging out together]. Six months after we met, we were rock stars. That was horrible."

Less hyped were the Steve Miller Band, who'd formed in November, 1966 in Berkeley, where Miller had onced played on a visit from his native Texas. The band's rise was nonetheless meteoric: A week after forming they were playing the Forum on Telegraph Avenue, and not long after that were booked by Chet Helms for the Avalon. At heart a blues fanatic, Miller was soon tailoring his sound to fit the Haight ambience, incorporating ragas into their repertoire. "I knew I couldn't miss," said Miller. "The Dead and the Airplane barely knew how to tune up at the time; the big highlight was playing "In The Midnight Hour" out of tune for forty-five minutes. It took me no time at all to put together a band that could play songs—in tune and tight."

Top: Skip Spence. Bottom: Wild-card singer-guitarist with Moby Grape. From left: Spence, Bob Mosley, Peter Lewis, Jerry Miller, Don Stevenson.

Along with the new bands came a revolutionary new radio format on the FM waveband. In February, 1967, deejay Larry Miller started playing underground rock tracks on his all-night show on KMPX; in April, Tom Donahue took over an earlier slot on the station. By the summer, KMPX was broadcasting hippie music twenty-four hours a day—much to the distaste of conservative programmers like Bill Drake, who wouldn't add Country Joe and the Fish's "Not So Sweet Lorraine" to his KHJ playlist in L.A. despite the fact that it had hit No. 1 on his San Francisco station. Drake claimed that the San Francisco "scene" was a myth, "magnifying itself basically on fumes." To Big Daddy, Bill Drake was retarding the country's pop music.

As the "Summer of Love" became a reality, the outside world moved in for the kill. *Time* put together a special issue, and *Life* ran a major feature entitled "The New Rock: Music That's Hooked the Whole Vibrating World." Hollywood churned out exploitation movies like Roger Corman's *The Trip* and Sam Katzman's *The Love-Ins.* By April, the Gray Line bus company was including a "Hippie Hop" tour of the Haight among its San Francisco attractions. Kids were swarming into San Francisco *en masse,* many of them panhandling for money, some taking part-time jobs like mail-sorting. Along Haight Street there was a permanent "revue" of hippie performers. "There will always be at least one man with long hair and sunglasses playing a wooden pipe," wrote Hunter S. Thompson in the *New York Times Magazine* in May. "[And] a hairy blond fellow wearing a Black Bart cowboy hat playing bongos...and a dazed-looking girl wearing a blouse but no bra." Drugs, Thompson concluded, had made formal entertainment obsolete in the "Hashbury."

Also swarming into the Haight, unfortunately, were all manner of creepy and nefarious characters: Dealers, cultists, general leeches. The

The reality of the "Summer of Love." The Gray Line bus company included a "Hippie Hop" tour of the Haight among its San Francisco attractions.

Haight-Ashbury Research Project, launched the following year, calculated that 15 percent of the people who'd drifted into the area in 1967 were "psychotic fringe and religious obsessives." When budding Hollywood groupie Pamela Des Barres checked out the Haight in January, she hung out with a street freak called "Bummer Bob," who played bouzouki in an outfit known as the Chamber Orkustra. Later he would be better known as Charles Manson acolyte Bobby Beausoleil. (Manson himself spent time in the Haight, allegedly living on the roof of the Straight Theater and recruiting a few damaged hippie chicks to his retinue while he was there. Sandy Good had been one of the original Deadheads at the Acid Tests and the Trips Festival.)

Two months later, writer Joan Didion visited from Los Angeles and was alarmed by the pervasive sense of menace in the community. As she noted in her famous piece "Slouching Towards Bethlehem," drug users were already forsaking acid for the joys of shooting crystal methedrine; those who *were* still tripping were having a lot of bummers. Where there was crystal meth, moreover, heroin soon followed to cushion the comedown: Even Emmett Grogan started messing with smack in the summer (he would die of an overdose on the New York City subway on April Fool's Day, 1978). For Didion, quoting from Yeats' famous poem "The Second Coming," "the center was not holding."

Among the various tensions beginning to surface in the Haight as spring turned into summer and the population swelled was a new friction between white hippies and black residents of the Fillmore district that lay to the south. Black teenagers accosted white longhairs who wandered through their neighborhood and sometimes physically attacked them. Beat veteran Chester Anderson, who published a regular bulletin with the title *Com/co,* called the Haight "the first segregated bohemia I've ever seen." More generally, Anderson could report that

Top: CIA agents keep a close eye on the Panhandle. Bottom: Something is happening, and you don't know what it is...

LOVE IS OUR LAW - TRUTH IS OUR WOR-
SHIP - FORM IS OUR MANIFESTATION
CONSCIENCE IS OUR GUIDE - PEACE
IS OUR SHELTER - NATURE IS OUR
COMPANION - ORDER IS OUR ATTITUDE
BEAUTY AND PERFECTION IS OUR LIFE

ONE LEAF AT A TIME

PATRIOTIC

"rape is as common as bullshit on Haight Street," and that "minds and bodies are being maimed as we watch, a scale model of Vietnam." Hepatitis and gonorrhea were spreading; health inspectors, worried about epidemics, issued a violation warning to a Digger crash pad. The Diggers themselves had taken to carrying guns around, and Com/co announced that "An Armed Man Is a Free Man." Love was the password in the Hashbury, noted Hunter Thompson, "but paranoia is the style." Elder statesmen like Gary Snyder were already recommending that hippies "tribalize" and live communally outside the city.

Five months after the "hippietopian" promise of the Human Be-In, Country Joe and the Fish manager Ed Denson admitted that he was "very pessimistic" about the hippie movement. "Right now it's good for a lot of people," he said, "but I have to look back at the Berkeley scene. There was a tremendous optimism there too, but look where all that went. The Beat Generation? Where are they now? What about hula-hoops? Maybe this hippie thing is more than a fad...but I'm not optimistic. If the hippies were more realistic they'd stand a better chance of surviving."

For his part, police chief Cahill—the man who'd actually coined the corny phrase "the love generation"—was more blunt.

"Hippies are no asset to the community," he said. "These people do not have the courage to face the realities of life."

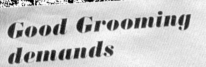

Good Grooming
demands

hair products

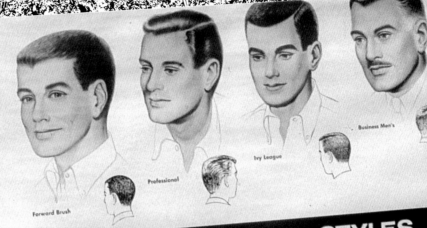

Forward Brush

Professional

Ivy League

Business Men's

OFFICIAL HAIR STYLES
for
MEN and BOYS

We specializ
in cutting hai
correctly . .
the way yo
like

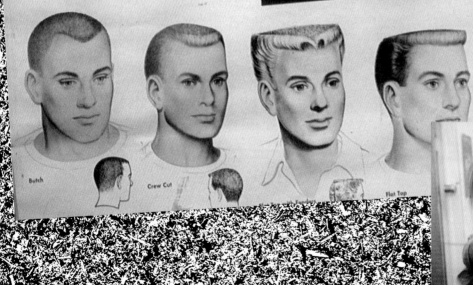

Butch

Crew Cut

Flat Top

Summer of Love, Death of Hippie

"OF ALL THE SHIFTY SCHEMES AND SCALY EXPLOITATIONS OF THE HOUR," noted Rock Scully, **"THE MONTEREY POP FESTIVAL IS THE MOST NEFARIOUS."** The Grateful Dead manager's reaction to the news that a consortium of L.A. movers and shakers was planning to stage an "international" pop festival at the Monterey fairgrounds 100 miles south of San Francisco was hardly atypical. The festival, dreamed or scammed up by John Phillips of the Mamas and the Papas and his producer/label-owner Lou Adler, was a bold attempt to bring together the very different music scenes of northern and southern California, **AND IT WAS GUARANTEED TO RUB SAN FRANCISCO UP THE WRONG WAY.**

Inspired directly by the Human Be-In in Golden Gate Park, Monterey Pop was perceived by the Bay Area bands as the most flagrant of Hollywood cash-ins—an attempt to ride on the coattails of a far more vibrant and organic music scene. "Traveling up the Coast from the

ruins of the Sunset Strip to the Haight is a Dante-esque ascent," Richard Goldstein had written in the *Village Voice.* "Those 400 miles mark the difference between a neon wasteland and the most important underground in the nation." Ralph Gleason would have agreed: For this "trench-coated conscience of San Francisco rock" (as he would be described in the Monterey Festival program), the so-called "freaks" of Los Angeles were "fostered and nurtured by L.A. music hype," whereas "what's going on here is natural and real."

"You'd have to say that San Francisco had the jump on L.A. in terms of drugs and psychedelia," says the writer Carl Gottlieb, then a member of North Beach satirical troupe The Committee. "There was a schism between north and south. Southern California was perceived by us in the north as plastic imitation of the real thing. We felt superior because we were actually living it. To the L.A. people, on the other hand, girls in San Francisco didn't shave under their arms and we were all granola-heads." It was a reprise of the old Freaks vs. Hippies battle, one waged with particular relish by Frank Zappa on the withering Mothers of Invention album *We're Only In It for the Money.* Nor was it an exclusively northern vs. southern Californian battle: When the Velvet Underground played the Fillmore in May, they were appalled by the supposed "tribalism" of hippie culture. "If you didn't smile a lot in San Francisco, they got very hostile towards you," said Factory film director Paul Morrissey, who was part of the Velvets' entourage. At the Fillmore, the band clashed with Bill Graham, who called them—and this from a man who'd grown up in the Bronx!—"disgusting germs from New York."

The Diggers predicted that Monterey would be a "rich man's festival," failing to convey the point that "the San Francisco bands... don't look on themselves as separated from the community, but live in

> Hollywood and Vine, Los Angeles: "Southern California was perceived by us in the north as a plastic imitation of the real thing."

the streets." The bands themselves were offended by the pseudo-hipness of John Phillips and the rest of the L.A. contingent. "The southern California and L.A. entertainment business entered into the scene with the 'San Francisco Wear a Flower in Your Hair' attitude," said Joe McDonald. "[It was] a total ethical sellout of everything we'd dreamed of." To Warner's head Joe Smith, many years later, McDonald added that it was as though "an entire new West Coast music community" had been created in the space of a month: "I mean, they just shoved us out there with everybody else, like we were part of this new childhood Zen. Somehow, the whole thing drained us. Sucked us dry. Maybe it was the pressure and hysteria and reality of Big Business vs. the Aquarian Age."

Ralph J. Gleason, "trench-coated conscience of San Francisco rock" and co-founder of *Rolling Stone*.

"The San Francisco bands had a very bad taste in their mouths about L.A. commercialism," admits Lou Adler. "And it's true that we were a business-minded industry. It wasn't a hobby. They called it slick, and I'd have to agree with them. We couldn't find the link. Every time John Phillips and I went up there, it was a fight—almost a physical fight on occasions. And that was right up to the opening day of the festival, with the Dead—the Ungrateful Dead, we called them—threatening to do an alternative festival." It was only thanks to the intercession of such neutral parties as Paul Simon, David Crosby, and publicist Derek Taylor that the San Franciscans were able to trust Adler and Phillips enough to agree to be part of the festival.

Preceded the previous weekend by the Fantasy Faire and Magic Mountain Music Festival in Mill Valley—featuring the Airplane and Country Joe and the Fish alongside such non-Bay Area acts as the Byrds, the Doors, and Smokey Robinson and the Miracles—Monterey Pop took place on the weekend of 16/18 June and brought together the cream of the American and British music scenes: The Who, the Jimi

Hendrix Experience, Otis Redding, the Butterfield Blues Band, Simon and Garfunkel, and many more. The San Francisco bands included the Dead, the Airplane, Country Joe and the Fish, Big Brother and the Holding Company, the Steve Miller Band, Moby Grape, and the Quicksilver Messenger Service—several of whom did indeed also play at an "alternative" free festival at nearby Monterey Peninsula College, with food provided gratis by the Diggers. The undoubted star of Monterey was Janis Joplin, who so wowed the crowd with her spine-chilling rendition of "Ball and Chain" that Big Brother was asked to play again the next afternoon in order that they could be filmed.

For the more cynical onlookers, Monterey was little more than a trade fair for the rapidly expanding music business. It was where the cannier pop moguls saw just how huge rock was going to become, where Bob Dylan's manager Albert Grossman hovered predatorily around Janis Joplin and even offered Columbia's Clive Davis a $100,000 package consisting of Quicksilver, Steve Miller, and the Electric Flag—despite having no connection to two of those bands.

Jann Wenner, publisher of *Rolling Stone*, in the magazine's San Francisco offices.

"As soon as the TV cameras screwed down on it, the vampire began to drink," noted Robert Hunter, who was about to commence work as a lyricist for the Grateful Dead. "Only those with self-contained blood units survived intact. It was ugly to watch the efficiency with which that scene was dismantled. 'The Abyssinians came down like wolves upon the fold.' There was no bone worth picking not stripped clean and the marrow sucked." Less histrionically, Monterey was a pivotal moment—the birth of the rock industry as we know it today. In the words of Jann Wenner, "It was the nexus: It sprang from what the Beatles began and from it sprang what followed."

If Monterey was the beginning of the acid era for the world at large, it was the beginning of the end for San Francisco itself. Stars were born

and deals were made, but the festival corrupted the innocence of the Bay Area's ballroom scene forever. By the late summer, bands like the Jefferson Airplane were starting to act like the rock stars they really were, rather than the community troubadours they'd pretended to be. Messianic standard-bearers the Airplane might have been, but friction was beginning to develop as allegiances and stylistic preferences asserted themselves within the band. Grace Slick and Spencer Dryden, who had been lovers for some months, were now a unit unto themselves in the group. Jack Casady and Jorma Kaukonen secretly longed to be Jack Bruce and Eric Clapton, belittling Marty Balin for his plaintive ballads. It didn't help that cocaine had arrived on the scene at Monterey, making everyone, in Paul Kantner's words, "ruder and nastier and colder and badder."

Ron Thelin closes the Psychedelic Shop in the autumn of love.

It was in this tumultuous state that the Airplane journeyed down to L.A. once more to start work on a new album—an insanely ambitious drug opus designed to top *Sergeant Pepper,* no less. They lived in a Bel Air mansion by day and got fired up on nitrous oxide by night, so the making of *After Bathing at Baxter's* was pure dementia. "It was absolutely crazy," recalled manager Bill Thompson. "Nude swimming going on all the time; Jorma firing his gun in the pool; kids sneaking through the doors looking for the Beatles…"

Overleaf: The Diggers' "Death of Hippie" march along Haight Street. "The media cast nets, create bags for the identity-hungry to climb in."

"Baxter's was our first psychedelic album, just because of the jamming," claimed Jorma Kaukonen. "At that time we were getting into the technology of learning how to play electric instruments in the style that became our benchmark, and that was the first album where Jack and I really started to stretch out." Seven months and $60,000 later, the Airplane had a costly flop on their hands—an album that, for all its drug-crazed inventiveness, never came close to repeating the success of *Surrealistic Pillow.*

Back in the Haight, where the Straight Theater had recently opened as a kind of funky, community-oriented alternative to the Avalon and Fillmore ballrooms, the Grateful Dead was dealing with the fallout from a major drug bust at 710 Ashbury. Pictures of the band post-bust appeared in the very first issue of *Rolling Stone.* Meanwhile they had acquired a second drummer/percussionist in the form of Mickey Hart and were attempting to work on their second album—described to Joe Smith as "a musical interpretation of an LSD trip." In November, the group abandoned the studio and taped some live shows at the Shrine Auditorium in L.A.—the first stage in a process that would lead to *Anthem of the Sun.*

Robert Crumb, the brilliant cartoonist whose work perfectly captured the demented spirit of the times.

In November, too, Big Brother and the Holding Company finally parted company with Julius Karpen and made overtures to Albert Grossman, the fearsome "Gray Cloud" behind the mystique of Bob Dylan and the sheer success of several other acts. "We were just so jazzed at the thought of Albert managing us, lowly *us,*" confessed Dave Getz; little did he guess that Grossman was interested in only one thing, and that was Janis Joplin. Grossman promptly signed the band to Columbia, the label to which Dylan had been signed since 1961. Monterey led to deals for other San Francisco bands that fall: Quicksilver and the Steve Miller Band both signed to Capitol Records for sizeable advances in November.

If you looked at San Francisco comically at this point, it could be said to have resembled a hippie cartoon: The Furry Freak Brothers, perhaps, or a *Zap* comic by Robert Crumb, the brilliant artist whose work appeared in *Ramparts* magazine and would grace the cover of Big Brother and the Holding Company's *Cheap Thrills* the following year. If you looked at the city soberly, however, it was turning into a pressure cooker of malevolent forces—a frightening, paranoid community of the

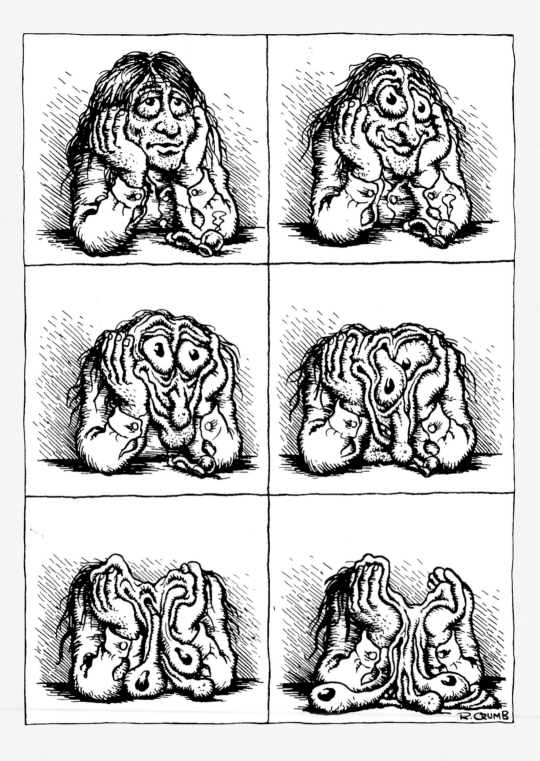

kind depicted in Philip K. Dick's *A Scanner Darkly*. In August, the dealer John Kent "Shob" Carter was stabbed to death by a disturbed acid casualty: His hand had been amputated, probably because his money briefcase had been cuffed to it. Three days later, the body of another dealer, "Superspade," was found tossed over a hillside in Marin County. In September, Kenneth Anger's *Lucifer Rising* was screened at the Straight Theater, with a soundtrack by "Bummer" Bobby Beausoleil and his Chamber Orkustra.

On October 6, 1967, a year after the "Love Pageant Rally" in the Hashbury, the Diggers organized a "Death of Hippie" march along Haight Street, a parade that concluded with the burial of the sign which had hung outside the Psychedelic Shop. "The media cast nets, create bags for the identity-hungry to climb in," the Digger press release ranted. "Your face on TV, your style immortalized without soul…the **free man** vomits his images and laughs in the clouds…" Within months, the Thelin brothers had departed the Haight, along with Allen Cohen and Michael Bowen. Emmett Grogan returned to New York, while other Diggers moved up to the Morning Star ranch (a.k.a. the Digger Farm) owned by Lou Gottlieb.

A general exodus from Haight-Ashbury was beginning, as people left to "get it together in the country" in the hippie communes. What

"Stoned Agin'," by Robert Crumb.

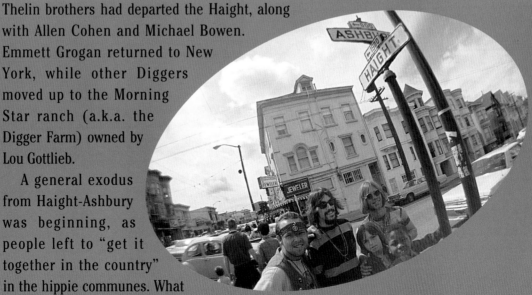

Bill Graham called the "general hope" of the Haight's heyday had died. **In the words of Derek Taylor—who'd enjoyed a blissful trip at Monterey on Owsley's "Purple Haze"—**

Hey, kid, don't bogart that joint...

"people always fuck up in the end."

CHAPTER 3
PURPLE HAZE

CHILDREN OF THE FUTURE

"When the San Francisco sound became popular, the band became the focal point. But it's more than that. It's party, the whole picture. The element of party has continually diminished as rock became big business."

CHET HELMS

BY EARLY 1968 HIPPIE CULTURE, DILUTED BY popular phenomena such as the musical *Hair*, had long since developed its own somewhat tiresome mannerisms. Expressions like "FAR OUT," "WHERE IT'S AT," "GETTING YOUR SHIT TOGETHER," and so on, served as a pat code. Names like Sky and Rainbird had become the order of the day. In the words of Owsley Stanley III, "the character of the thing had changed." The idyll of

the Haight as a place where bands and fans merged into a collective entity, transcending their egos and sharing their lives in what Hank Harrison called "dehierarchized, leaderless family structures," was drawing to a close. Some groups assumed the aristocratic airs that musicians in other cities—London, New York, Los Angeles—had long maintained. Instead of losing themselves in the anonymous psychedelic throng of the ballrooms, fans stood around mesmerized, fearful of missing a stroke of the lead guitarist's pick. Shows were no longer participatory ceremonies, living theater, electric music for the mind and body. "We were now applauding the *presence* of the artist, rather than the performance," noted Joshua White, the principal light show artist at the Fillmore East theater Bill Graham opened in New York in February 1968. This was the birth of rock idolization. Eric Clapton was God.

Quicksilver in the studio with producer Harvey Brooks. From left: Cipollina, Duncan, Brooks, Freiberg, Elmore.

To some of the Bay Area musicians, the change was confusing. Gary Duncan of Quicksilver couldn't understand why "sometimes I play really shitty and it doesn't make any difference at all." Jerry Garcia was more cynical about the way ritual had been turned into rote. "The Acid Tests have come down to playing in a hall and having a light show," he told Hank Harrison. "It's watching television, loud, large television. Like [Bill] Graham, he was at the Trips Festival and all he saw was a light show and a band. Take the two and you got a formula. It is stuck, man, hasn't blown a new mind in years…"

In an attempt to offer an alternative to the "formula" of the Fillmore, the Dead, the Airplane, and Quicksilver joined forces and took over the lease of the old Carousel Ballroom on the corner of Market Street and Van Ness Avenue. The first gig in the new venue, costarring Quicksilver and the Dead, was on January 17, 1968, with the official opening marked a few weeks later by a Dead/Country Joe

The Family Dog

AVALON BALLROOM   FRI·SAT·SUN·OCTOBER·27·28·29   DANCE·CONCERT·LIGHTS·IBIS

and the Fish double-header. The venue might have lasted longer than the six months it did if the Dead's business advisor, a Wall Street broker named Ron Rakow, hadn't negotiated the most crippling rental agreement in rock history. By the summer, in another of his "getting up early in the morning" coups, Bill Graham had taken over the venue and renamed it the Fillmore West.

The Dead, meanwhile, were struggling to capture the essence of their sound on tape. With engineer Dan Healy, they used equipment bought by Owsley to record several live shows in the early part of 1968—in particular, the shows they played on the "Quick and the Dead" tour, a hike up the Pacific northwest coast with Quicksilver in January. They had long since given up on recording in the studio: After an aborted session in New York the previous November, Dave Hassinger vowed never to work with them again.

Quicksilver Messenger Service at the Avalon Ballroom.

The subsequent task of editing these live tapes into *Anthem of the Sun* was a daunting one, and brought to the boil what Rock Scully described as "a tug-of-war between experimentation and just plain songs." Both Jerry Garcia and Phil Lesh wanted to push things sonically as far as they would go—on the four-section "That's It For The Other One," the band came perilously close to prog-rock—and even tried to fire the more bar-band oriented Pigpen and Bob Weir. In May, the Dead's great astral-rock signature song "Dark Star" was released as their second Warner Brothers single.

Quicksilver, too, opted to make their second album a live recording. On their first sessions for Capitol in the fall of '67 they had recorded an entire album with Nick Gravenites and Harvey Brooks, then junked it. "Quicksilver Messenger Service, oh boy," remembered beleaguered engineer Jay Ranellucci. "They spent two hundred hours in the studio, threw it all out and started over. The poor engineer

doesn't get a break, 'cause there's four of them in the band, with each guy showing up wanting to redo his part. The smoke got pretty thick, too. Some Quicksilver mixing sessions, you didn't dare walk into the room; you'd get a contact high immediately." The resulting *Quicksilver Messenger Service,* recorded in late '67 and early '68, was a pretty turgid affair as it was. Certainly the album never came close to capturing the visceral thrill of the quartet onstage, founded on the dual-guitar attack of John Cipollina and Gary Duncan.

In October, 1968, following the Dead's lead, Quicksilver recorded several performances at the Fillmore West and East, stitching together the results as *Happy Trails* of 1969. The album was an instant live classic: With an evocative cover designed by George Hunter, it caught better than anything else the intense, almost dangerous quality of San Francisco's ballroom sound. The entire first side was taken up by an epic six-part version of Bo Diddley's "Who Do You Love"—the ultimate expression of their Wild-Western, desperadoes-on-peyote vision, and one of the greatest sequences of live rock music ever put on record. Grounded in the primitive stomping of Elmore and Freiberg, the interplay between Duncan's chugging rhythm guitar and Cipollina's livid, quivering lead was thrilling and hypnotic.

A third San Francisco band, Big Brother and the Holding Company, opted to go the live route in 1968. The strategy made sense, given the raw charisma of Janis Joplin onstage. Janis lived for the power that performance gave her: She said that playing live was equivalent to a hundred orgasms—quite a statement from someone so highly sexed. Joplin's exhibitionism was really just a cover for her fragility: Onstage, she could act out and eroticize her pain. The only drawback was Big Brother itself, whom many critics thought a clunky millstone

Janis in November, 1967: "They wanted to see her shoot up, they wanted to see her scream and yell and screech about."

173

round her neck: "The band drags her at every turn," complained Jon Landau.

Columbia staff producer John Simon was inclined to agree. After a disastrous attempt to record them live in Detroit in March, 1968, he switched to Columbia's own studio in New York but felt frustrated both by the band's ineptness and by Joplin's surprising lack of spontaneity. "She was planning out every single moan and shriek," he said later. With almost the whole group sliding perilously into heroin addiction, Simon did his best to salvage something from the wreckage, though he asked for his name to be taken off the credits. The result was an album originally entitled *Sex, Dope, and Cheap Thrills,* later abbreviated at Columbia's insistence to *Cheap Thrills.*

Big Brother and Santana at the Fillmore West.

The first side of *Cheap Thrills,* at least, made up in raw excitement for what it lacked in musical finesse. Joplin's frantic vocals played only too happily to the expectations of fans who were becoming voyeuristic to the point of ghoulishness. As ex-boyfriend Country Joe said after her death, "they wanted to see her shoot up, they wanted to see her get loud, they wanted to see her scream and yell and screech about."

"What was happening," her biographer Myra Friedman noted astutely, "was that Janis was actually being merchandized as the symbol of everything that was against the very idea of merchandizing." As it turned out, even Joplin was tiring of Big Brother—despite the massive success of *Cheap Thrills,* a No. 1 album for eight weeks after its release in August, 1968. Deep down, she wanted to do something altogether more soulful and credible. She wanted to be Etta James, Tina Turner, even Otis Redding—"to be respected as a great singer and not as a hippie freak," in the words of Nick Gravenites. After a last Big Brother show at the Avalon on

December 1, she split, essentially to become the solo artist Albert Grossman had always wanted her to be.

Meanwhile Joplin's great rival for the crown as San Francisco's rock queen, Grace Slick, was drinking almost as heavily as Janis. Slick may have hailed from the high society of Palo Alto rather than the oil refineries of Port Arthur, Texas, but she was no less susceptible to liquor. In May, 1968, the Airplane bought a seventeen-room mansion at 2400 Fulton Street, on the very edge of Golden Gate Park, and transformed it into the ultimate hippie rock palace: 710 Ashbury was cute by comparison. The factions within the band were proving as divisive as ever—Casady and Kaukonen were busy planning the side project that would become Hot Tuna—and Marty Balin felt himself slowly being squeezed out of the picture. "Around the time of *Baxter's*," he remembered bitterly, "I realized everybody was off their ass and didn't give a shit about anybody or anything else. So I lost interest."

In the early summer, they recorded *Crown of Creation*, described by Paul Kantner as "a political reaction to the forces around us as the Haight-Ashbury got darker and the jack boots and the anti-dope and the crushing forces came in to squelch communism and whatever else was going on here..." Kantner also claimed that things were "getting out of hand and out of control a bit"—that the band was "getting a little too bold and expressive"—but after the self-assurance of *Pillow* and the crazy experiments of *Baxter's*, *Crown of Creation* merely sounded jaded. "Lather" was Slick's dig at her boyfriend Spencer Dryden ("Lather was thirty years old today/They took away all his toys"), and her version of David Crosby's "Triad" was the era's most wanton hymn to *ménages à trois*. But Kantner's Theodore Sturgeon-inspired title track was pretentious tripe, and Balin's songs sounded tired.

Big Brother and the Holding Company, June, 1968. From left: Dave Getz, Peter Albin, Janis Joplin, James Gurley, Sam Andrew.

After touring Europe with the Doors in September, the Airplane came home to San Francisco and threw an epic bash at the Fulton Street mansion that was attended by many of their Haight peers. The dinner was like a last supper of acid rock, belying the fact that most of the San Francisco bands had now left town. Back in March, the Grateful Dead had given a kind of "farewell" gig on Haight Street, playing four numbers on the back of a truck, with power wired from the Straight Theater. Others followed the bands out to communes in Marin County and Mendocino, or even further afield in Oregon and New Mexico. "The urban scene kind of decentralized," said Peter Coyote. "What happened was that there were a series of way stations all up and down the coast from Happy Valley…to Whitethorn." The whole rock community was in retreat: Like Bob Dylan and the Band on the East Coast, it was pulling back from the madness it had unleashed and "woodshedding" in the country.

The end of the Haight's golden age was marked by the ousting of George Hunter from the Charlatans in April, 1968. After further attempts at capturing the band's magic on tape—at Golden State Recorders in July 1967 and at the Pacific High studio in early 1968—the Red Dog pioneers began to unravel. Dan Hicks formed his spin-off band the Hot Licks, playing tongue-in-cheek pre-Fifties' pop and releasing the album *Original Recordings.* Mike Ferguson was fired, and a new pianist added to the band. Finally, Richie Olsen and Mike Wilhelm informed George Hunter that the band was all over, though they actually soldiered on without him or Hicks and put together a new lineup of the band that signed to Philips. The resulting album was a travesty, and Olsen and Wilhelm knew it. Indeed, like the other original members, they knew that a series of bad decisions and missed opportunities had condemned the group to being a merely

Jorma and Jack jam on down, backstage before an Airplane gig.

local phenomenon. "We knew we had something," Olsen lamented. "There was an empty gnawing feeling that we didn't get to fulfill our destiny."

The same sort of thing was happening to Moby Grape, whose disintegration had begun with Skip Spence going off the deep end Brian Jones-style. In the summer of 1967 the group based themselves in Malibu and worked with David Rubinson on material for their second album. After four tracks had been recorded, however, Columbia insisted that they finish the record in New York, where they could be better supervised. (Only the pretty "He" survived from L.A.) Reconvening in Manhattan, they were talked into adding horns and strings to tracks like "Can't Be So Bad" but couldn't disguise the basic state of chaos that undermined *Wow* (which came with a free bonus album, *Grape Jam,* made up of blues tracks recorded with Al Kooper and Mike Bloomfield).

The Steve Miller Band. From left: Tim Davis, Jim Peterman, Boz Scaggs, Miller, Lonnie Turner.

Peter Lewis suffered a breakdown due to his collapsing marriage, while Skip Spence, having persuaded broadcasting veteran Arthur Godfrey to come down to the studio and play on the daft "Just Like Gene Autry: A Foxtrot," flipped out completely and tried to attack Jerry Miller with a fire-axe. Leaving the frazzled "Seeing" as a last desperate cry—with its exhortation "Save me! Save me!"—he was straitjacketed and carted off to Bellevue Hospital. "Skippy was a visionary," Don Stevenson remembered. "And what happened was he broke through. And part of him didn't want to compromise, come back and rejoin the rest of us." Was Spence, in the end, just another member of the "psychotic fringe" mentioned by the Haight-Ashbury Research Project?

A band in considerably better shape at this point was the one led by Steve Miller. Much less interested than his San Francisco peers in

181

the supposed "authenticity" of live performance, the Texan had no qualms about going to London early in 1968 to record *Children of the Future* with rising producer Glyn Johns. Now fleshed out by Miller's boyhood chum Boz Scaggs, the group seamlessly mixed downhome blues with ethereal, multilayered psychedelia. Even better was *Sailor,* again produced by Johns and released later that year, this has stood time's test as one of the great Bay Area albums.

Scaggs quit the band immediately after *Sailor's* release, heading over to Muscle Shoals, Alabama, to cut his first solo album, with *Rolling Stone* editor Jann Wenner, of all people, in the producer's chair. Interestingly, Scaggs is one of the few dissenting voices when it comes to nostalgia for Haight-Ashbury. "Much has been made of the so-called music community in San Francisco," he has remarked, "but to my knowledge there's never been a true community there.

It was never like L.A. or New York, where you can jump in a taxi and say, 'Take me over to so-and-so's session.' That never existed in San Francisco.

It was always this group or that group—the Airplane, the Dead— and I was never part of that scene." Tellingly, Scaggs would achieve his greatest success with a succession of mid-Seventies' albums recorded in Los Angeles—the rock Babylon scorned by so many San Francisco bands.

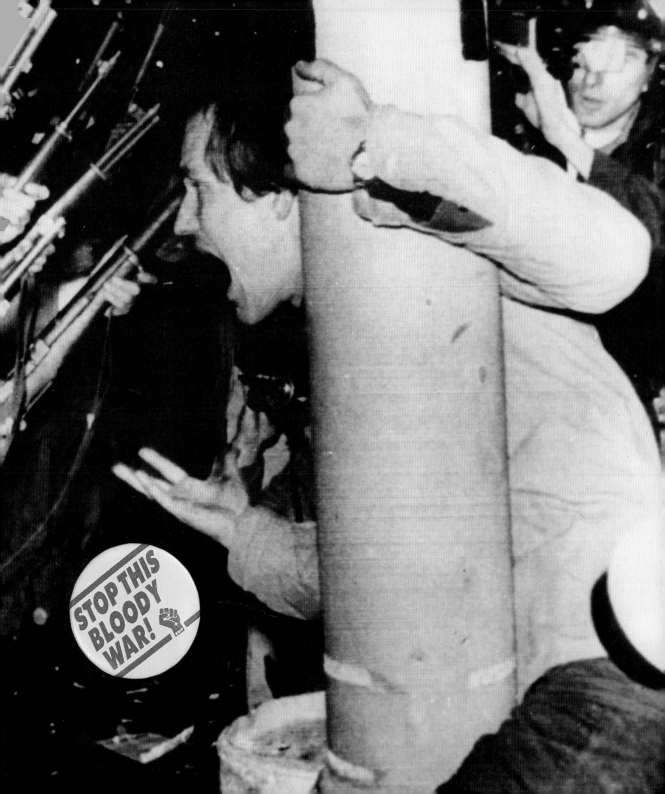

Beyond Acid

IF SUMMER 1967 WAS A SUMMER OF LOVE
—an arguable notion in any case—then summer 1968 was categorically a summer of hate. The year which began with the Tet Offensive in Vietnam turned into twelve months of riots, strikes, and protests all over the Western world. Campuses exploded in America and Europe. Martin Luther King was assassinated, and relations between blacks and whites in America were never the same again.

In the transition from flower children to street fighting men, the ideals of peace and love curdled horribly. Vietnam was still the principal focus of protest. Lyndon Johnson, Kennedy's successor and inheritor of the war, had raised the numbers of soldiers involved there to half a million, but more and more Americans viewed the war with disfavor, and a watershed was reached when the ugly facts about the massacre at My Lai began to emerge. There were major demonstrations in London: 25,000 people gathered in Grosvenor Square outside the U.S. Embassy. On the war front the soldiers themselves were war-sickened, homesick, and disillusioned. Draft avoidance had become an organized activity. New Left organizations, like Students for a Democratic Society,

continued to support nonviolent protest, but during 1968 the Weatherman Faction of the SDS began a terrorist campaign against the U.S. government. In October, they bombed a CIA building, an army recruiting station, and several police precincts. The hippie watchword was now "Up Against the Wall, Motherfucker!" Demonstrators at the National Democratic Convention in Chicago were brutally attacked by the Chicago police—under the direction of the city's reactionary Mayor Daley—and the seven and a half thousand U.S. troops that had been given riot control training for the occasion. The ensuing trial of the "Chicago Eight," concerning incitement to riot, was a dark farce.

Creedence Clearwater Revival, January, 1970. From left: Doug Clifford, Stu Cook, John Fogerty, Tom Fogerty.

Some of the San Francisco bands were cynical about "the revolution." Country Joe McDonald espoused an almost Dylanesque disdain for the rhetoric of the Youth International Party, or Yippies, going so far as to take out an ad in the *New York Times* accusing Jerry Rubin and Abbie Hoffman of irresponsible leadership at the convention. (Four months after the Human Be-In that brought the hippies and the Yippies together, former Berkeley activist Steve DeCanio had argued presciently that "this alliance between hippies and political radicals is bound to break up...there's too big a jump from the slogan of 'flower power' to the deadly realm of politics.")

Things were getting uglier in San Francisco itself. After Martin Luther King's assassination in Memphis on April 4, the racial tension in the Fillmore ghetto forced Bill Graham to think about moving out. Three months later, after a final Fillmore show, he took over the Carousel Ballroom from Ron Rakow and reopened it as the Fillmore West with a show by the Butterfield Blues Band and Ten Years After. Now he was spending most of his time commuting between San Francisco and New York, where the Fillmore East had opened with Big Brother and the Holding Company's East Coast debut in March.

"The more success Bill achieved, the more tense he became," recalled his second-in-command Paul Baratta, "[and] the more he started to be at odds with the Ralph Gleasons and Jann Wenners and the whole *Rolling Stone* establishment, as it were." Meanwhile Chet Helms, the impresario the *Rolling Stone* establishment preferred, was served an eviction notice on the Avalon Ballroom. The hippest rock venue in San Francisco finally closed in October.

Fortunately, new bands were coming up through the woodwork, helping to rejuvenate the Bay Area scene. From unglamorous El Cerrito came four nondescript-looking *schlubs* who'd variously called themselves the Golliwogs and the Blue Velvets and were now trading as the Creedence Clearwater Revival. "We were four guys from a small town, totally outside the mainstream of the record business," said John Fogerty, the band's singer and principal songwriter. "We did not have a Hollywood manager. We were not even on a Hollywood label. We were basically a PO Box, distribution-type deal, a rocket ship built in the basement that just exploded."

With their roots in the frat-party circuit in the East Bay, the band had latterly graduated to the less salubrious tittie bars of North Beach. But Fogerty was canny enough to keep one eye trained on hip Haight-Ashbury. "It's been said that what we were doing seemed very far removed from the rest of San Francisco, but that's not quite true," he has said. "'Suzie Q' was designed to fit right in. The eight-minute opus. Feedback. Like 'East-West.'" Furnished to FM radio, a tape of "Suzie Q" became a giant underground track in 1968, followed in January 1969 by the smash-hit "Proud Mary," and then the *Bayou Country* album.

Fogerty had never been near a bayou, let alone grown up in Louisiana. What he had done was steep himself in the blues and country music of the American South, and in all its mythological folklore. And what Creedence ended up sounding like was Little Richard or Solomon Burke fronting a redneck rockabilly band. Fogerty's songs—succinct snapshots of Southern life, along with full-throttle message numbers like "Fortunate Son"—reflected the turning away from psychedelia, back to rural Americana. In this, at least, they were in synch with with the Dylan of *John Wesley Harding*, the Band of *Music from Big Pink*, and the Stones of *Beggar's Banquet*.

Yet they remained quitessentially a blue-collar bar band, even when they were briefly outselling every other group in America, Cyril Jordan of the Flamin' Groovies joked that even when Creedence were at the peak of their fame they could shop at Safeway without being recognized, Creedence, wrote Ellen Willis, "never crossed the line from bestselling rock band to cultural icon...in some respects [Fogerty] resembled the solid, sustaining husband who is forever being betrayed for the dashing, undependable lover." Cyril Jordan of the Flamin' Groovies joked that even when Creedence were at the peak of their fame they could shop at Safeway without being recognized.

An altogether more exotic aggregation was Santana, formed by Mexican-born guitarist Carlos Santana. As a teenager in Tijuana, Carlos had checked out local R&B bands and been turned onto American blues guitar heroes like B.B. King. Playing in a band called the Strangers, he landed a regular gig at El Convoy. Reluctantly following his family to the Bay Area in 1963, he would make frequent trips back to Tijuana, where visiting black Americans taught him the chords to the latest B.B. King and Bobby "Blue" Bland hits. Back in San Francisco, he attended Mission High where older students turned him on to the white rock scene in Haight-Ashbury. Graduating in June 1965, he started hanging out on the streets of the Haight, panhandling and washing dishes to put food in his mouth.

Overleaf: Rear view of John Fogerty as Creedence ignite Oakland Coliseum in January, 1970.

One night, Butterfield and Bloomfield let the little Mexican kid jam with them, which led to an offer from Bill Graham for the band to play occasional support slots at the Fillmore. "We were playing songs like 'Mary Ann' by Ray Charles and 'Misty' and 'Taste of Honey,' only with Latin percussion," Santana told White. "To me, it still wasn't music. It was just a process of learning, you know." After a bout of tuberculosis in early 1967, Carlos pulled the band together and got serious.

Bill Graham, for one, became a major fan: "What impressed me is that it was an attempt at fusing rock and Afro and Latino and getting a rhythmic, sensuous sound into rock, which I've always thought it lacked in many cases." Manager Stan Marcum helped recruit bassist David Brown and organist Gregg Rolie. Instrumental in the percussive sound of numbers like "Jingo" was conga player Marcus Malone, the first of many Santana members to fall foul of the law when he went to jail for stabbing a girlfriend's husband to death.

After Ron Rakow booked them for the Carousel Ballroom, Santana made their Fillmore West debut in July, 1968. Soon they were being represented by Bill Graham's agency and even topping the bill at the Fillmore West—"the only band ever to headline there without having made a record," as Bill Graham recalled. After a tour with Crosby, Stills and Nash in 1969 broke them in the Midwest, Santana signed to Columbia and commenced work on their first album with David Rubinson (who'd worked not only with rock acts such as Moby Grape but had also produced Latin records by the likes of Mongo Santamaria.)

Boasting a Top 10 single in its version of Willie Bobo's "Evil Ways," Santana was an almost immediate hit, its sweet funk and sizzling syncopation breathing fresh air into the stagnant rock scene. Within a few bars of "Waiting," moreover, it was obvious that Carlos himself was an outstanding and completely individual player, burning up the fretboard and sustaining long, searing notes on his Gibson Les Paul. "You could not turn on the radio for six months without hearing the damn record," recalled Rubinson. "In the middle of all the vapid bullshit that was going on with psychedelia and mandala in 1969, here was the essence, boiled down to drums and percussion and pulse. It was just balls-out music, and that's what people wanted to hear. Guitar was unknown, voiced the way it was in Santana. The way they used the keyboard was completely different, almost like a Latin horn section, and there was no brass."

Venturing into the same polyrhythmic territory at this time—though without the overt Latin influence—was Sly Stone, the producer whose impatience had so intimidated the countless acts trooping through the portals of Autumn Records. It had long been Sly's secret dream to lead a band fulltime and break away from the drudgery of studio work. With his exposure to the freaky goings-on in Haight-Ashbury and his willingness to mix up rock and soul on his radio shows, it was almost inevitable that Sly and the Family Stone would be no ordinary band. In fact, they were more like a multiracial hippie soul troupe, bridging the gap between the Haight and the black scene in Oakland, birthplace of the Black Panthers. "We had all this input that no one had ever thrown together before," recalled drummer Greg Errico. "All of a sudden there were all these traditional influences that came to an intersection. You had R&B, you had white pop, you had the psychedelic thing, and the English thing, mixing together for the first time."

The Family Stone's Columbia debut, *A Whole New Thing,* stiffed so badly that A&R man David Kapralik urged them to simplify things on the next record. Sly took his advice and came back with the storming "Dance to the Music," as exciting a dance anthem as any made in the wake of Motown's great years. "What Sly had done was so simple it

might have occurred to almost any black kid living in the late Sixties in San Francisco," wrote Dave Marsh. "The antinomian spirit of R&B...was grafted on to the close-knit, deliberately-paced rock band experience; the musical wildness of the rock band then was wedded to the utter discipline of the soul group." *"Dance To The Music,"* in other words, pulverized the polarities of black and white, male and female, funk and rock—a whole new thang, indeed. The rest of the Dance to the Music album was almost as bold, built on the rock-solid grooves of drummer Errico and bassist Larry Graham and taking the listener ever higher with its blend of horns, keyboards, choppy guitar, and unisex vocals. This was James Brown via the Human Be-In.

Other bands were emerging at this time, too. The Sons of Champlin led a vogue for Bay Area white soul that would culminate in the formation of Tower of Power. It's A Beautiful Day were yet another group masterminded by the ignominious Matthew Katz, and whose sound was more than a little derivative of his original San Franciscan charges the Jefferson Airplane. The Owsley-managed Blue Cheer, whose *Vincebus Eruptum* was distinguished by a neanderthal version of Eddie Cochran's "Summertime Blues," were rapidly osmosing into San Francisco's very own Iron Butterfly. Bill Graham, having missed out on signing Santana to his newly-formed Fillmore label, would introduce the world to Tower of Power and Cold Blood.

The Grateful Dead had not quite forsaken the psychedelic dream, although *Aoxomoxoa* was something of a return to structure after the diffuse *Anthem of the Sun.* Recorded in the fall of '68 in a spanking-new sixteen-track studio in San Mateo, songs like "St. Stephen" and "China Cat Sunflower" boasted abstruse, allusive lyrics by Jerry Garcia's old crony Robert Hunter but were moving away from the spaciness of acid rock towards the friendlier, more countrified sound

Santana celebrate the success of their debut album with Columbia's Clive Davis. From left: Gregg Rolie, Chepito Areas, Michael Shrieve, Davis, David Brown, Carlos Santana, Michael Carabello.

of the band's early Seventies' albums.

Still, the Dead chose to leave one last timeless testament to the lysergic spirit of San Francisco in the Sixties with the double *Live/Dead*, featuring the definitive extended version of "Dark Star"—that veritable Holy Grail of psychedelia which Deadheads term "the zone." Recorded at the Carousel Ballroom in late February/early March, 1969, *Live/Dead* seems to draw a kind of curtain on the Haight era, especially since the Dead themselves were now firmly established in the hills of Marin County, far from a Haight-Ashbury that had become, in Charles Perry's words, "a heroin-infested slum where somebody could get knifed for a bag of groceries." "Those of us who'd grown up [in the scene] got out," recalls Bob Weir. "One reason in particular was bathtub methedrine. I knew plenty of musicians who were screwed up by methedrine. They lost their teeth, they lost their sense of humor. Some of them turned to crime. It did a nasty number on people, because methedrine had a nasty comedown and many users turned to heroin."

Like Laurel Canyon down in Los Angeles, Marin County had become a whole scene unto itself—what Myra Friedman called "one unrelenting group-grope." As in Laurel Canyon, musicians slept with each other's "old ladies," got wasted all night, and lived a high old life in their mountain hideaways. "Living in this scene, it's like too many pretty cats, too many parties, too much dope, too much alcohol," said Nancy Getz, wife of Big Brother's Dave Getz. "Everybody has done so much with so many people that nobody ever gets it together, like, to live with one person. And those cats in Marin, they want a chick who stays home and polishes doorknobs all day and is real dumb to live with, not to have a good time with. So yeah, you go into the Trident [in Sausalito] and you see someone and you ball him again and you go around and just get it on all the time. It's just gettin' it on—because you get so lonely."

Sly Stone at the Monterey Jazz Festival, September, 1969.

MAD

THE SONS

MAD RIVER

THE SONS OF CHAMPLIN

FRUMIOUS BANDERSNATCH

FRUMIOUS

4/c for 3/2

No one had ever imagined heroin would become such a problem in the rock community: Big Brother themselves had been decimated by the drug. In July, 1969, James Gurley's wife Nancy tragically died of an overdose while the couple were camping with their child. Post-Big Brother, Janis Joplin's heroin use was obscured by her basic alcoholism but only grew with her chronic insecurity and self-loathing as she tooled around Larkspur picking up those "pretty cats." Bad reviews for the first San Francisco gigs with her new Kozmic Blues Band in March, 1969, further fueled her self-destructiveness, and the chaotic sessions for *I Got Dem Ol' Kozmic Blues Again, Mama* hardly improved matters. The hubris of her disastrous appearance as the sole white artist at the Stax-Volt Christmas show in Memphis the previous December continued to haunt her.

Latecomers to the San Francisco party: Mad River, the Sons of Champlin, Frumious Bandersnatch.

Only the Jefferson Airplane continued to base themselves in the city, holding court at Fulton Street and recording *Volunteers* at the new Wally Heider studio on Hyde Street. For all Paul Kantner's pressing for a more militant attitude on the album—"Up against the wall, motherfucker!" was the title track's famous exhortation—the group was drowning in cocaine and Porsches. Spencer Dryden was drinking himself senseless since Grace Slick had moved on to Kantner; in April, 1970, he would be replaced on drums by Joey Covington. "Once it clicked," recalled Marty Balin, "everyone was free and they were their own leaders and did whatever they wanted to do, and that democracy immediately destroyed it." One night, while the Airplane was opening a live set with "Volunteers," Balin looked round at the band as he was singing and saw that "there was such futility in the togetherness of these people and their political understanding of what we were all about that I had no further wish to be associated with it." In April, 1971, he would leave the band he had formed six years before.

Quicksilver Messenger Service were also going through a rocky patch. After a show at Winterland on New Year's Eve, 1968, Gary Duncan made up his mind to quit the band and hit the road with Dino Valente, the veteran folkie who had at one time been set to sing with Quicksilver. In the charismatic, potentate-like Valente Duncan appeared to have found the elder brother he'd never had, and both men fancied themselves as hippie outlaws, easy riders on the rock'n'roll highway. They spent much of 1969 "motorcycling out," in Duncan's words, hoovering drugs and spilling their seed from coast to coast. Quicksilver, meanwhile, found a new lease of life when the English session pianist Nicky Hopkins, a veteran of the London R&B scene, joined the band. Hopkins had played with the Steve Miller Band in London, moving to San Francisco as a result and guesting on the Airplane's *Volunteers*. Duncan and Valente dropped by to see Quicksilver one evening that fall and began to criticize the lameness of their new music. By the end of the year, they were both in the band, with Valente more or less taking over lead vocals from David Freiberg.

A **TYRANNICAL** AND **BULLYING** FIGURE, Valente persuaded the band to fly to Hawaii and record their next album in a plantation overlooking Pearl Harbor, using a portable studio built by the Dead's old engineer Dan Healy. During their stay on the island, he succeeded in ALIENATING ALMOST EVERYONE INVOLVED in the album, BRANDISHING GUNS and **PSYCHING OUT** those who had the temerity to disagree with him. A MUSICAL CHARLATAN OF THE MOST BRAZEN KIND, he so INTIMIDATED Nicky Hopkins that the mild-mannered pianist was forced to leave the band. Manager Ron Polte made the same decision shortly afterward. By October, 1970, even John Cipollina had left Quicksilver Messenger Service.

The Dead play Golden Gate Park, 1970. From left: Pigpen, Garcia, Weir.

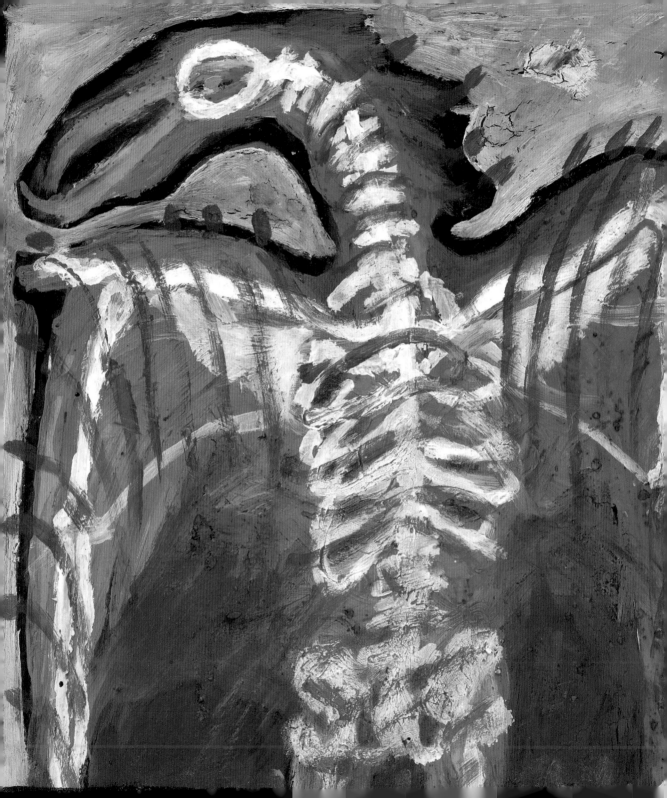

Luv'n'Haight

<u>"THIS WAS NOT THE BEAUTIFUL PLACE I'D expected," said an English girl who visited Haight-Ashbury in 1968. "There were no flowers, or peace, or love. The streets were tatty, the people looked dead. Too many wasted addicts hanging around. Kids with their eyes glazed over and their faces old. Doreen and I joined in the life a bit. We went to the local hospital to give blood because we could earn £8 [$22] a pint for our best blue English blood. The waiting room was full of addicts who were turned back because of hepatitis, or because they'd given blood in the last three months. They looked filthy and sad."</u>

Slowly but surely, the Haight was being left behind by the rest of the world. While the Airplane were buying their Fulton Street mansion, the student population of Paris, supported by many of the citizens, was mounting an insurrection which for one heady moment looked as if it might turn into a fullscale revolution. Students in Prague had a tougher time: In August the USSR invaded Czechoslovakia to put a stop to Dubcek's increasing liberalization of the country. Jan Palic, twenty-one, immolated himself in the process.

By early 1969, America's hippie culture spiralled out

205

of control. The Manson killings in Los Angeles signalled that apparently gentle longhairs who talked of peace and love might actually be psychopathic—that "dropout" culture had attracted all manner of dangerous inadequates along the way. Yet at the same time the desire to join together was strong enough for half a million longhairs to congregate on a farm in upstate New York in August, 1969.

Woodstock may have been on the East Coast, but the tenor of the festival was set, as it had been at Monterey, by acts from San Francisco: Not so much Janis Joplin or the Grateful Dead, who both performed poorly, but Santana and Sly and the Family Stone, together with Country Joe McDonald and his historic "F-U-C-K" cheer. When Sly sang that he wanted to take the hippies higher and Santana electrified the crowd with "Soul Sacrifice," they gave acid rock the multiracial, Afro-Latin-American jolt it needed.

Jefferson Airplane, meanwhile, were forced to play at seven in the morning, waking the stoned tribes with a rousing version of "Volunteers." "Alright, friends, you have seen the heavy groups," announced Grace Slick; "now you will see morning maniac music..." "Our slot was supposed to be 9:00 P.M. the night before, but it was typical hippie organization," recalled Paul Kantner. "Time wasn't of consequence. Half the crew was asleep or naked in the pond, and I remember the film cameras were pointing in the sky half the time."

Back in San Francisco, Quicksilver manager Ron Polte had dreamed up what he intended to be California's very own Woodstock—the so-called "Wild West Festival," to be held in Golden Gate Park with eight stages and all the big Bay Area acts (the Dead, Janis Joplin, Quicksilver, the Airplane, Country Joe and the Fish, Santana, Sly and the Family Stone, the Steve Miller Band) playing. But Polte hadn't allowed for a number of bureaucratic hurdles, or for the various radical groups who were pressuring him to make the festival free. This was a time when you couldn't win: You couldn't please the establishment, and you couldn't please the anti-establishment either. "We live in a world where people are afraid, where people are paranoid," said Tom Donahue, whose experience as a promoter Polte had drawn on but who at the time was too enmired in cocaine to be of much use. Ten days before the festival was due to start on August 22, it was cancelled.

At the very end of the year—at the very end of the decade—San Francisco did get its own Woodstock, but it turned out to be a very different beast from the three-day summer bash in the Catskill Mountains. It came partly out of a suggestion by Dead co-manager Rock Scully that the Rolling Stones conclude their 1969 tour of America—a tour which had seen them lambasted for high ticket prices—with a free concert in Golden Gate Park. The Stones agreed it was a good idea, but couldn't get permission to play in the park. At the last minute, the only venue available was a godforsaken speedway stadium in the scraggy brown hills across the Bay, east of San Francisco: Altamont. "It was like a moonscape of crushed auto bodies," said Owsley Stanley; "it looked like a skull, and I thought, 'This place smells of death.'" Jerry Garcia recalled that Emmett Grogan referred to the upcoming event as "the First Annual Charlie Manson Death Festival."

Taking the advice of the San Francisco bands, the Stones hired the Hell's Angels to act as security for the concert on December 6. They'd used Angels to protect the stage at the free London concert they'd given in Hyde Park, and figured that these greasy beasts would be the same kind of people. They were sorely mistaken. Little did they know that there had been escalating gang and biker violence in and around Oakland in the weeks leading up to Altamont, or that there was intense rivalry between some of the chapters hired. The Stones bought into the

Overleaf: The morning before the nightmare that was Altamont, December, 1969.

207

same romance with the Angels that the San Francisco bands had maintained ever since the heyday of the Merry Pranksters. (Only months before Altamont, a *Rolling Stone* reporter was gushing that the Angels "embody the primordial energies of brute force, the excremental vision, and the freedom of the outcast...they are magnificent incarnations of the beast in all of us.")

Up against the reality of the Angels' proletarian power trip, the bourgeois bohemians of San Francisco's failed Eden were helpless. From Santana's opening set that day, the ogres in denim and leather went into action, stomping innocent peaceful people with a wild rage. After the Airplane started their set with an optimistic "We Can Be Together," Marty Balin upbraided the Angels for their brutality and was punched unconscious for his pains. Grace Slick attempted to calm things down in a pathetic prefiguration of Mick Jagger's impotent pleas later that night. "Woodstock was a bunch of stupid slobs in the mud and Altamont was a bunch of *angry* slobs in the mud," she reflected later. The Grateful Dead opted not to play at all, writing "New Speedway Boogie" about the experience instead.

What was interesting was how the San Francisco bands and scenesters chose to single out Mick Jagger as the prime culprit at Altamont. "It was here that the vital flaw, laziness disguised as integrity, first showed up," wrote Grateful Dead insider Hank Harrison. "It was here that the idealistic little San Francisco bands made the mistake of inviting, and underestimating, the immense ego of Mick Jagger and the Rolling Stones." The problem, it turned out, wasn't the latent psychopathic tendencies of the average Hell's Angel, it was the arrogance of these satanic rock stars from London. Perhaps it was even the sin of stardom itself.

"What right does this god have to descend on this country in this way?" asked Bill Graham, a man who would later promote several of the Stones' American tours. Rock Scully, whose suggestion the concert had been in the first place, argued that if the Stones "hadn't been so cut-throat, then Bill Graham would certainly have been involved in Altamont and it would have worked out a lot better." The fact that Altamont (especially as depicted in the Maysles brothers" riveting film *Gimme Shelter*) exposed to plain view just how naively ill-prepared the Stones were to deal with such a situation was ignored.

Scully was closer to the truth when he said, in *Living with the Dead,* that Woodstock and Altamont were "two ends of the same mucky stick...the result of the same disease: The bloating of mass bohemia in the late Sixties." The Stones' flirtation with the devil was the same thing as the San Francisco bands' sympathy with the Angels: It was decadence presented as radical chic. And when the Angels stabbed Meredith Hunter to death that night, mere feet below the becaped Mick Jagger, it brought the paranoid psychedelic frenzy of San Francisco in the Sixties to an inevitable climax.

"In truth," wrote Robert Draper in *The Rolling Stone Story,* "San Francisco had been rushing kamikaze-style toward the disaster that became Altamont, hell-bent for an explosive finale...[the first wave bands] were now America's, not just San Francisco's, and all this talk about a second wave of talent...was wishful. The Bay Area's soil still contained the minerals for sprouting greatness, as Creedence Clearwater Revival proved. But that same garden was cluttered with weedy impostors: Blue Cheer, Womb, Mother Earth, and a host of others."

For Bill Graham, San Francisco never fully recovered from Altamont: He said later that "we've never been able to wipe that stain from our record." As the new decade began, psychedelia went into retreat. There

was a gradual mellowing of the West Coast sound, as though people needed to be healed after Manson and Altamont. The Grateful Dead, encouraged by David Crosby, began pursuing the country-rock sound of *Workingman's Dead* and *American Beauty,* both recorded early in 1970. "We convince ourselves that these secondhand, down-home, grits-eatin' roots connect to our youthful, folksy, bluegrassy, jug-bandy, coffeehouse selves," wrote Rock Scully. Every Wednesday night, Jerry Garcia would take a pedal steel guitar down to his old stamping ground in Menlo Park to play country songs with his old friend John "Marmaduke" Dawson. Out of these little gigs was born a Dead spinoff band called the New Riders of the Purple Sage.

The Dead retreat into Marin County country-rock, with a little help from the New Riders of the Purple Sage.

Things were less mellow at the Airplane mansion. "As we all got a little bit older, the thing we were doing that was fun—which was playing music—became a career," says Jorma Kaukonen. "From the vantage point of thirty years later, it's my impression that it's hard to keep an artists' community together, especially when you go from living in a one-room apartment to being able to buy almost anything you want. It's hard to keep a focus on what it was that brought you that opportunity." Kaukonen and Casady's Hot Tuna was now a going commercial concern, and Paul Kantner released a solo song cycle, *Blows Against the Empire,* that drew on his increasing fascination with science fiction and led eventually to the birth of the post-Airplane Jefferson Starship.

Kantner and Slick eventually fled the coop and moved to Bolinas in Marin County, where they had a baby girl in January 1971. Motherhood was to make little difference to Slick's drinking: That May she nearly died in a car crash as she swerved drunkenly off the road on the approach to the Golden Gate Bridge. On *Bark,* released after Marty Balin's departure from the group, a song called "Third Week at the

Chelsea" summed up their collective inertia and depression. "It was a bad time," recalled Bill Thompson, who was still managing them after all this time. "Nobody was working together; nobody was playing together. It was kind of the end, even if it didn't really die."

Even this was nothing compared to what was going on in the Santana camp. Around Carlos Santana swirled such a blur of guns and drugs and Black Panthers that the guitarist began to keep his distance from his own group. In 1970, junkie pianist Alberto Gianquinto turned Dave Brown and Stan Marcum onto heroin, and the drug spread through the band like a bad rash. Carlos butted heads with both Gregg Rolie and Michael Carabello, and when percussionist Coke Escovedo joined the group, the others thought he was turning Carlos against them. Marcum thought Carlos' sanctimoniousness on the subjects of sex and drugs hypocritical, while Carlos was "starting to feel weak and resentful towards the band because I was demanding more."

Amazing, then, that in the midst of all this the group managed to record the classic *Abraxas,* an album that remained at No. 1 for six straight weeks and produced the sublime hit version of Fleetwood Mac's "Black Magic Woman." A remarkable advance on the group's debut, *Abraxas* was a magical, sensual collection of songs and instrumentals that spoke of Carlos' growing interest in spirituality and gave his spine-tingling guitar playing even greater range.

Drugs were finally getting the better of Janis Joplin as *Abraxas* made its way to the top of the charts in September, 1970. In April, the singer had dispensed with her Kozmic Blues Band and put together the much stronger Full Tilt Boogie Band, but it hadn't stopped her ceaseless quest for oblivion. During the summer, the anachronistic good-time-gal persona of "Pearl" started to take her over; she even began talking in a different voice. At her Larkspur home it was party time twenty-four hours a day, open house to every conceivable form of leech and slimeball.

"She had people she'd bring into the house and then she'd bitch because she was giving them bed and board," remembered Kris Kristofferson, who tore around with her and Bobby Neuwirth during a two-week spree and who was just another of the "pretty cats" with whom Janis was smitten. When her old Austin friend Chet Helms ran into her at a Grateful Dead show in July, he thought she looked like something out of *The Naked Lunch.*

At least Joplin was able to channel her persona into one last decent album, the posthumously released *Pearl.* Starting work on the record in Los Angeles at the beginning of September, she gave producer Paul Rothchild her all on versions of Garnett Mimms' "Cry Baby" and "My Baby," along with Howard Tate's "Get It While You Can," all three of them classic New York soul ballads from the Berns and Ragovoy stable. The mood of the record was balanced precariously between Kris Kristofferson's wistful "Me and Bobby McGee" (a No. 1 single the following year), and the desolate Dan Penn/Spooner Oldham ballad "A Woman Left Lonely," with funkier material like "Half Moon" wedged in between them.

No one was really sure why, during the sessions, Joplin started using heroin again, other than because junkies invariably do start using heroin again. She was making the music she'd always wanted to make. She'd recently begun a relationship with a trust-fund renegade called Seth Morgan. She was even talking about marriage, for chrissakes. In the early hours of Sunday, October 4, in the Landmark Hotel in Hollywood, Janis had one last hit of smack before bedtime. The time of her death was estimated at 1:40 A.M.

The Fillmore West, like the Fillmore East shortly before it, opened its

215

doors for the last time in the summer of 1971. Second-wave San Francisco acts like Cold Blood, Elvin Bishop, It's a Beautiful Day, and even the Flamin' Groovies whetted the crowd's appetite for Creedence Clearwater Revival, who were playing for the first time as a trio without the just-departed Tom Fogerty, and for the headlining Santana. Bill Graham, loudly bemoaning "the unreasonable and totally destructive inflation of the live concert scene," also claimed that "the heavy use of drugs and need to escape by young people is one of the reasons I'm backing away from this business." *The Last Days of the Fillmore* documentary, released in May, 1972, featured a classic scene in which Graham exploded in a fit of hysterical rage at ex-Charlatan Mike Wilhelm.

The end of the dream: The Haight becomes the haunt of junkies and runaways.

By 1973, San Francisco was all but dead as a music town: As *Rolling Stone's* Michael Lydon put it, "the machine managed to make San Francisco an outpost of itself." In 1975, a year in which both Ralph Gleason and Tom Donahue died, Jann Wenner packed up his *Rolling Stone* staff and moved to New York. San Francisco, he claimed, was "a provincial backwater."

Bill Graham continued to rule as the czar of the Bay Area's live scene, but it wasn't with anything as exciting as the ballrooms of the Sixties. In the summer of 1991 I drove up to the spanking-new Shoreline Amphitheater in Mountain View to interview him for a book I was writing about The Band. As he walked me up to his office, with its grandstand view of the auditorium, he told me the venue was "the culmination of all my dreams." In the background, the sound of the Grateful Dead rumbled away as it had done so many times at the Fillmore. Nearly a quarter century after he'd first put them onstage, the band Hank Harrison rightly called "the single most popular unknown rock group in the world" were still raking it in, still playing long,

meandering jams for their tie-dyed Deadhead followers. Some of these kids, I figured, must have been the children of the original hippies who'd filled the Fillmore.

And now both Bill Graham and Jerry Garcia are dead.

When an interviewer once asked Jerry Garcia about the "lost innocence" of the Haight-Ashbury era, the Grateful Dead's unofficial leader replied that "it wasn't that innocent"—that "our own background was sort of that deeply cynical beatnik space which evolved into something nicer with the advent of psychedelics."

The point was a good one: That San Francisco's psychedelic rock scene wasn't founded on naivety but on the explosive poetry of the Beats and the inspired irresponsibility of the Pranksters. That Haight-Ashbury was less about floating around with flowers in your hair than about breaking through to reality via Rimbaud's "derangement of the senses." What was naive about the Haight—about the golden "Summer of Love" that lasted roughly from the fall of 1965 to the spring of 1967—was the belief that it would last, or even that it would have any lasting effect on people's politics.

"I thought that, with an incredible amount of media blitzkrieg and books and knowledge, you could change people," said Grace Slick. "But you can't. The only person I can change is me." A study of "protest rock" between 1966 and 1970 even reached the conclusion that "rock music may have channelled social unrest into a more politically passive direction…by helping to translate revolutionary opinions into rhetorical cant, protest rock facilitated token opposition to the status quo among youth…"

"Ultimately, we found out the hard way by having our innocence smashed out of us," said Country Joe McDonald. "Lots of things

happened, mainly political assassinations and war. You can't separate the era from that, from all those caskets. Ours was an era of extremes, unbelievable extremes. And inside that era we were like this little dreamland."

When the era was over, the lucky few whose brains weren't scrambled went back to the drawing board and figured out ways of dealing with the new reality of the music business.

"You either snorted cocaine and shot heroin," says Carlos Santana, "or you folded your hands and THANKED GOD."

BIBLIOGRAPHY

Cream Puff War issues 1 and 2

DEROGATIS, Jim,
Kaleidoscope Eyes
(Citadel Underground, Secaucus N.J. 1996)

DRAPER, Robert,
The Rolling Stone Story
(Mainstream, Edinburgh 1990)

FRAME, Pete,
The Complete Family Trees
(Omnibus, London 1993)

FRIEDMAN, Myra,
Buried Alive: The Biography of Janis Joplin
(William Morrow, New York 1973)

ANTHONY, Gene,
*The Summer of Love: Haight-Ashbury
at Its Highest*
(Last Gasp, San Francisco 1980)

GLATT, John,
*Rage and Roll: Bill Graham and
the Selling of Rock*
(Birch Lane Press, New York 1993)

GLEASON, Ralph J.,
*Jefferson Airplane and the
San Francisco Sound*
(Ballantine, New York 1968)

GOLDSTEIN, Richard,
Goldstein's Greatest Hits
(Prentice-Hall, Englewood Cliffs N.J. 1970)

GRAHAM, Bill, with GREENFIELD, Robert
*Bill Graham Presents:
My Life Inside Rock and Out*
(William Morrow, New York 1993)

GREENFIELD, Robert,
*Dark Star: An Oral Biography of
Jerry Garcia*
(William Morrow, New York 1996)

GRUSHKIN, Paul D.
The Art of Rock
(Artabras, New York 1987)

HARRISON, Hank,
The Dead
(Celestial Arts, Millbrae Calif. 1980)

JOYNSON, Vernon,
*Fuzz, Acid and Flowers: A Comprehensive
Guide to American Garage, Psychedelia and
Hippie Rock 1964–1975*
(Borderline, Telford, England 1993)

KANTNER, Paul,
*A Guide Through the Chaos (A Road to the
Passion): The Spoken Word History of the
Jefferson Airplane and Beyond*
(MonsterSounds CD, 1996)

LEE, Martin A., and SHLAIN, Bruce,
*Acid Dreams: The CIA, LSD
and the Sixties Rebellion*
(Grove Press, New York 1985)

LYDON, Michael,
Rock Folk
(Dial Press, New York 1971)

OBST, Lynda Roben (ed.),
The Sixties
(Rolling Stone Press, New York 1977)

PERRY, Charles,
The Haight-Ashbury: A History
(Vintage, New York 1985)

ROWES, Barbara,
Grace Slick: The Biography
(Doubleday, New York 1980)

SCULATTI, Gene, and SEAY, Davin,
*San Franciscan Nights: The Psychedelic Music
Trip 1965–1968*
(Sidgwick & Jackson, London 1985)

SCULLY, Rock, with DALTON, David
Living With The Dead
(Little, Brown, Boston 1996)

SELVIN, Joel,
*Summer of Love: The Inside Story of LSD,
Rock and Roll, Free Love and High Times
in the Wild West*
(Plume/Penguin, New York 1995)

SELVIN, Joel,
San Francisco: The Musical History Tour
(Chronicle Books, San Francisco 1996)

SMITH, Joe,
Off the Record
(Sidgwick & Jackson, London 1989)

STEVENS, Jay,
*Storming Heaven: LSD and the
American Dream*
(Heinemann, London 1988)

THOMPSON, Hunter S.,
"The 'Hashbury' is the Capital of the Hippies,"
New York Times Magazine,
May 14, 1967

WOLFE, Tom,
The Electric Kool-Aid Acid Test
(Farrar, Straus & Giroux, New York 1968)

INDEX

Acid Tests 59-63, 75-7, 91, 121-3, 145, 169
Adams, Carolyn 91
Adler, Lou 149, 153
Aguilar, Dave 57
Albin, Peter 27, 63, 176
Albin, Rod 27, 63, 115
Alpert, Richard 35, 118
Altamont 207-11
Anderson, Chester 145
Anderson, Ray 83
Anderson, Signe Toly 47, 50, 91, 111-14
Andrew, Sam 63, 83, 176
Anger, Kenneth 163
Anonymous Artists of America 123
Arbuckle, Fatty 11
Areas, Chepito 196
Autumn Records 53-5, 99-101, 109, 195
Avalon Ballroom 17, 78, 80, 81-5, 89, 95, 105, 115, 133, 139, 141, 175, 190

Babbs, Ken 33-5, 61, 77, 91, 123
Balin, Marty 47, 50, 89-91, 97, 111, 112, 137, 157, 177, 201, 210, 213
Band 191
Banham, Reyner 97
Baratta, Paul 190
Barthol, Bruce 70
Beach Boys 97
Beatles 39, 40, 97, 103-5
Beats 9, 15, 23-5, 24, 31, 37, 147, 219
Beau Brummels 53, 55, 57
Beausoleil, Bobby 145, 163
Berg, Peter 67
Berkeley 69-73, 70, 118, 129-31, 147
Bess, Donovan 121
Big Brother & the Holding Company 11, 27, 63, 79, 83, 85, 89, 105-7, 118, 132, 155, 161, 173-5, 174, 176, 189, 201
Bishop, Elvin 217
Blackhawk 23, 27
Bloomfield, Mike 181
Blue Cheer 197, 211
Blues Project 81
Boise, Ron 77
Boone, Steve 115
Bowen, Michael 87, 118, 119, 163
Brand, Stewart 75, 77
Brautigan, Richard 119, 121
Brooks, Harvey 168, 171
Brown, David 194, 196, 214
Bruce, Lenny 25
Buckley, Lord 25
Buddha 131
Buffalo Springfield 139
Burroughs, William 23, 25, 45
Butterfield Blues Band 79, 81, 155, 189
Byrds 47, 153

Cabale 73
Cannon, Gus 93
Carabello, Michael 196, 214
Cargill, Melissa 91
Carousel Ballroom 169, 189, 194, 199
Carpenter, John 79, 81
Carter, John Kent "Shob" 163
Casady, Jack 50, 111, 112, 157, 177, 178, 213
Caserta, Peggy 37, 94
Cassady, Carolyn 9-11
Cassady, Neal 9-11, 31, 32, 61, 79, 109, 121, 123-5
Castell, Luria 114
Chamber Orkustra 145, 163
Charlatans 15, 37, 41-7, 44, 46,
62, 63, 65, 77, 85, 89, 99, 114-15, 117, 120, 179-81
Chicago Democratic Convention 189
Chocolate Watch Band 56, 57
Cipollina, John 47, 65, 95, 96, 124, 168, 173, 203
Clifford, Doug 188
Coasters 114
Cohen, Allen 87, 118, 163
Cohen, David 70, 132
Cold Blood 197, 217
Com/co 145-7
The Committee 151
Conklin, Lee 85
Cook, Stu 188
Corman, Roger 143
Country Joe and the Fish 15, 39, 73, 131-2, 143, 147, 153, 155, 169-71
Covington, Joey 201
Coyote, Peter 125, 179
Creedence Clearwater Revival 188, 190-1, 192, 211, 217
Crosby, David 153, 177, 213
Crosby, Stills and Nash 194
Crumb, Robert 160, 161, 162

Davis, Clive 155, 196
Davis, Ronny 67
Davis, Tim 180
Dawson, John "Marmaduke" 213
The Dead (Harrison) 11
"Death of Hippie" march 163
DeCanio, Steve 189
Denson, Ed 147
Des Barres, Pamela 145
Dick, Philip K. 163
Didion, Joan 145
Diggers 118-19, 147, 151, 155, 163
Donahue, Tom 53-5, 54, 99, 101, 109, 134-5, 143, 207, 217
Doors 153, 179
Drake, Bill 143
Draper, Robert 211
Dryden, Spencer 50, 87, 111, 112, 157, 177, 201
Duncan, Gary 65, 95, 96, 97, 168, 169, 173, 203
Dupont, Bard 98
Dylan, Bob 2, 21, 39, 161, 179, 191

Electric Flag 155
The Electric Kool-Aid Acid Test (Wolfe) 121
Elliott, Ron 53
Elmore, Greg 65, 95, 96, 168, 173
Erickson, Roky 105
Errico, Greg 195, 197
Errico, Jan 101
Escovedo, Coke 214

Family Dog 35, 47, 62, 63-5, 75-7, 81, 83, 85, 170
Fantasy Faire 153
Ferguson, Mike 37, 44, 45, 85, 114, 117, 179
Ferlinghetti, Lawrence 11, 23, 131
Fillmore 47, 69, 75-7, 81-3, 85, 89, 95, 111, 125-7, 139, 145, 151, 169, 189
Fillmore East 169, 173, 189
Fillmore label 197
Fillmore West 171, 173, 189, 194, 215-17
Final Solution 59, 60
Flamin' Groovies 55, 57, 115, 217
Fogerty, John 188, 190-1, 192
Fogerty, Tom 188, 217
Fosselius, Ernie 59, 60
Free Speech Movement 69-71
Freeman, Bobby 53
Freiberg, David 27, 47, 95, 96, 168, 173, 203
Fricke, David 139-41
Fried, Bob 85

Friedman, Myra 89, 175, 199
Frond, Bevis 17
Frumious Bandersnatch 200
Fugs 67-9, 83
Full Tilt Boogie Band 214

Garcia, Jerry 27, 29, 33, 39-41, 59, 61, 64, 75, 91-3, 94, 108, 111, 133, 169, 171, 202, 207, 213, 219
Getz, Dave 161, 176
Getz, Nancy 199
Gianquinto, Alberto 214
Ginsberg, Allen 11, 21, 22, 23-5, 31, 61, 69, 119, 131
Gleason, Ralph J. 51, 65, 89, 97, 118, 151, 152, 190, 217
God Street Wine 17
Godfrey, Arthur 181
Golden Gate Park 58, 118, 119, 129-31, 130, 144, 149, 202, 206, 207
Panhandle 118, 119, 130, 144
Goldstein, Richard 97, 151
Good, Sandy 145
Gorky's Zygotic Mynci 17
Gottlieb, Carl 151
Gottlieb, Lou 163
Graham, Bill 57, 66, 67-9, 79-85, 89, 115, 121, 125-7, 126, 151, 165, 169, 171, 189-90, 194, 197, 211, 217-19
Graham, Bonnie 85
Graham, Larry 195
Grateful Dead 15, 57, 63, 64, 69, 77, 80, 85, 91-3, 94, 107-11, 108, 115, 118, 121, 130, 133, 153, 155, 161, 169-71, 179, 197-9, 202, 206, 210, 212, 213, 217-19; see also Warlocks
Gravenites, Nick 171, 175
Great Society 65, 69, 81, 89, 99-101, 100, 111, 133
Greene, Herb 63
Griffin, Rick 47, 85, 129
Grogan, Emmett 119, 145, 163, 207
Grossman, Albert 81, 155, 161, 177
Gunning, John Francis 70
Gurley, James 63, 107, 176
Gurley, Nancy 107, 201
Guthrie, Woody 73

Haight-Ashbury Free Clinic 87
Haight-Ashbury Legal Organization (HALO) 109
Haight-Ashbury Research Project 145, 181
Hair 167
Ham, Bill 45, 83
Harmon, Ellen 35, 47, 63
Harrison, Hank 11, 169, 210, 217
Hart, Mickey 161
Harvey, Bob 47
Hassinger, Dave 133, 171
Healy, Dan 109, 171, 203
Hell's Angels 58, 59-61, 71, 121, 207-11
Helms, Chet 9, 25, 47, 57, 62, 63-5, 77, 78, 79-85, 97, 105, 111, 121, 141, 167, 190, 215
Hendrix, Jimi 153-5
Hicks, Dan 45, 115, 116, 117, 179
Hoffman, Abbie 189
Hoffmann, Albert 31, 37
Hollingsworth, Ambrose 95
Holzman, Jac 139
Hopkins, Lightnin' 127
Hopkins, Nicky 203
Hot Licks 179
Hot Tuna 177, 213
Howl (Ginsberg) 11, 23
"Human Be-In" 118, 124, 129-31, 147, 189, 189
hungry i 25, 27, 55
Hunter, George 37, 41-5, 44, 85, 114, 116, 117, 120, 173, 179
Hunter, Meredith 211

Hunter, Robert 27, 29, 155, 197

Instant Action Jug Band 73
Iron Butterfly 197
It's A Beautiful Day 197, 217

Jabberwock 73
Jackson, Ginger 47
Jacobsen, Erik 114-15
Jagger, Mick 210
Jazz Workshop 23
Jefferson Airplane 15, 47-51, 50, 65, 67, 79, 89-91, 97, 111-14, 127, 133-7, 153-7, 169, 177-9, 178, 201-6, 210, 213-14
Jefferson Starship 213
Johns, Glyn 47
Joplin, Janis 9, 11, 19, 25, 27, 63, 104, 105-7, 106, 132-3, 155, 161, 172, 173-7, 176, 201, 206, 214-15
Jordan, Cyril 55, 57, 115, 191

Kantner, Paul 27-9, 47, 50, 81, 91, 97, 111, 112, 114, 127, 157, 177, 201, 206, 213
Kapralik, David 195
Karpen, Julius 132, 161
Katz, Matthew 51, 89, 137-9, 197
Katzman, Sam 143
Kaukonen, Jorma 27, 47, 50, 91, 93, 112, 137, 157, 177, 178, 213
Kelley, Alton 47, 63, 80, 85
Kennedy, John F. 28
Kerouac, Jack 11, 23, 31
Kerr, Clark 71
Kesey, Ken 29-35, 59, 61, 71, 75, 79, 91, 119, 121-5
King, Al 41
King, Martin Luther 187, 189
Kingston Trio 27
KMPX 134-5, 143
Knickerbocker, Bob 59
Knight Riders 55
Kooper, Al 181
Kozmic Blues Band 201, 214
Kraemer, Peter 115
Krassner, Paul 79
Kreutzmann, Bill 39-41, 64, 94, 108
Kristofferson, Kris 215
Krug, Peter 73
Kula Shaker 17

Lagunitas 107, 132
La Honda 33, 59
Landau, John 175
Larkspur 95, 201, 214
The Last Days of Fillmore 217
Laughlin, Chandler 45
League for Spiritual Discovery 35
Leary, Timothy 35, 38, 124, 131
Lennon, John 105
Lesh, Phil 41, 63, 64, 93, 94, 108, 171
Levine, Steve 131
Lewis, Peter 137-41, 140, 181
Liberty Hall Aristocrats 27
Life 91, 143
Linde, Sam 44
Living with the Dead (Scully) 211
Locks, Seymour 83
Longshoremen's Hall 63, 65, 77, 115
Los Angeles 91, 97, 103, 149-53, 150, 183
The Love-Ins 143
"Love Pageant Rally" 115-18, 163
Lovell, Vic 31
Lovin' Spoonful 65, 97, 114, 115
Lucifer Rising 163
Lydon, Michael 95, 217

McClure, Michael 21, 23, 121
McDonald, Country Joe 70, 73, 97, 131-2, 153, 175, 189, 206, 219
McKernan, Ron (Pigpen) 27, 39-41,

64, 94, 107-9, 108, 171, 202
MacNeil, Terry 115
Mad River 200
Magic Mountain Music Festival 153
Magic Theater for Madmen Only 37, 45
Mainliners 45
Malone, Marcus 194
Manson, Charles 145, 206
Marbles 65
Marcum, Stan 194, 214
Marin County 199, 213
Marsh, David 197
Martin, Tony 83
Matrix 51
Melton, Barry 39, 70, 73, 107, 132
Menlo Park 29, 39, 213
Mercury Rev 17
Merry Pranksters 15, 32, 33-5, 59, 61, 75-9, 91, 119, 121-5, 210, 219
Miller, Jerry 137, 140, 141, 181
Miller, Larry 143
Miller, Stanley, see Mouse, S.
Miller, Steve 137, 138, 141, 180, 181-3
Mime Troupe 55, 65-9, 68, 77, 81, 83
Miner, David 98
Mitchell, Bobby 53-5, 101
Mnasidika 37, 87, 94
Moby Grape 15, 137-41, 140, 155, 181, 194
Mojo Men 55, 56, 57, 101
Monterey Pop Festival 99, 149-57, 161, 165
Morgan, Dana Jr 39-41
Morgan, Seth 215
Morrissey, Paul 151
Moscoso, Victor 85
Mosley, Bob 137, 139, 140
Mother's 55, 99
Mothers of Invention 65, 151
Mouse, Stanley 63, 80, 85
Murcott, Billy 119
Murray, Jimmy 95, 96, 124
Mystery Trend 56, 59, 67, 69

Nagle, Ron 59
Nelson, David 27
Neuwirth, Bobby 215
New Riders of the Purple Sage 213
New York 169, 189
New York Times 189
New York Times Magazine 143
North Beach 9, 23, 25, 27, 37, 95, 190
Novato 93

Off Stage 29
Olema 95
Olivia Tremor Control 17

Olsen, Richie 41, 44, 115, 117, 137, 179-81
On the Road (Kerouac) 11, 25, 31
One Flew Over the Cuckoo's Nest (Kesey) 31, 33

Palao, Alec 45, 114
Palic, Jan 205
Palo Alto 29, 31, 33, 39
Parrish, Maxfield 41
Paul Revere and the Raiders 55
Perry, Charles 75, 93, 118, 131, 199
Perry Lane 31-3
Peterman, Jim 180
Phillips, John 149, 153
Phish 17
Polte, Ron 95, 203, 206-7
Pranksters, see Merry Pranksters
Presley, Elvis 21, 23
The Psychedelic Experience (Leary & Alpert) 35
Psychedelic Shop 87, 90, 156, 163
Purple Onion 25

Quicksilver Messenger Service 15, 27, 65, 89, 93-5, 96, 124, 137, 155, 161, 168, 169, 171-3, 203

Rakow, Ron 171, 189, 194
Ramparts 161
Ranellucci, Jay 171
"Rebirth of the Haight/Death of Money, Now" march 119
Red Dog Saloon 45-7, 46, 85
Redding, Otis 127, 155
Rexroth, Kenneth 21, 23
Rohan, Brian 109
Rolie, Gregg 57, 194, 196, 214
Rolling Stone 65, 95, 154, 161, 190, 210, 217
Rolling Stone Story (Draper) 211
Rolling Stones 41, 191, 207-11
Romero, Elias 83
Rothchild, Paul 139, 215
Rubin, Jerry 118, 131, 189
Rubinson, David 55, 81, 125, 139, 181, 194-5
Rusted Root 17

Sahl, Mort 25
San Francisco Oracle 87, 118, 129, 131, 133
"San Francisco - The New Liver-pool" 80
San Francisco State 37, 41, 59
San José 75
Sanders, Ed 83
Santamaria, Mongo 194
Santana 174, 191-5, 196, 197, 206, 210, 214, 217
Santana, Carlos 191-5, 196, 214, 221
Sausalito 139, 199

Savage, John 15-17
Savio, Mario 71
Scaggs, Boz 180, 183
A Scanner Darkly (Dick) 163
Schiller, Larry 91
Sculatti, Gene 55, 101
Scully, Rock 63, 75-7, 93, 103, 109, 129, 149, 171, 207, 211, 213
Scully, Tim 91
Sebastian, John 97
"The Seed" poster 85
Selvin, Joel 65
Sender, Ramon 77
Shad, Bobby 107
Shapiro, Mike 57
Shaw, Greg 15
Shelter 27
Shoreline Amphitheater 217
Shrieve, Michael 196
Simon, John 175
Simon, Paul 153
Simon and Garfunkel 155
Simpson, David 109
"Skull and Roses" poster 80
Slick, Darby 39, 47, 98, 99, 111
Slick, Grace 29, 65, 98, 99, 111-14, 112, 113, 137, 157, 177, 201, 206, 210, 213, 219
Slick, Jerry 98, 99, 111
Sly & the Family Stone 195-7, 206
Smith, Dr. David 87
Smith, Joe 109, 153, 161
Smokey Robinson & the Miracles 153
Snyder, Gary 21, 25, 131, 147
Solidarity Day march 42-3
Sometimes a Great Notion (Kesey) 35
Sons of Champlin 197, 200
Sopwith Camel 115
"Sounds of the Trips Festival" 89
Sparrow 139
Spectrum: Songs for Owsley 17
Spence, Skip 47, 87, 111, 137-41, 140, 181
Spiritualized 17
Stanford University 31, 33
Stanley, Owsley III 17, 61, 75, 79, 91-3, 167, 171, 197, 207
Stax-Volt Christmas show 201
Steve Miller Band 137, 138, 141, 155, 161, 180, 181-3, 203
Stevenson, Don 137, 140, 181
Stewart, Sylvester 53
Stills, Steve 139
Stone, Sly 57, 99-101, 114, 195-7, 198
Strachwitz, Chris 73
Straight Theater 145, 161, 163
Summer of Love (Selvin) 65
Syndicate of Sound 56, 57

Tangent 29
Taylor, Derek 153, 165

Ten Years After 189
Thelin, Jay 87, 90, 119, 163
Thelin, Ron 87, 90, 119, 156, 163
13th Floor Elevators 105
Thompson, Bill 111, 127, 157, 214
Thompson, Hunter S. 143, 147
Thornton, Willie Mae 133
Tikis 55
Time 103, 143
Tower of Power 197
Town Criers 47
Townshend, Pete 125
"A Tribal Stomp" 79
"Tributes" 65, 71
The Trip 143
Trips Festival 76, 77-9, 85, 145, 169
Turner, Lonnie 180

Unobsky, Mark 45

Valente, Dino 29, 94-5, 203
Valentino, Sal 53
Van Meter, Ben 83
Vejtables 55, 57, 101
Velvet Underground 151
Vietnam 187
Village Voice 11, 151
Virginia City 45-7

Warlocks 39-41, 59, 61-3
Wavy Gravy's Hog Farm 123
Weathermen 189
Weinberg, Jack 71
Weir, Bob 39, 64, 79, 94, 95, 108, 171, 199, 202
Wells, Junior 127
Wenner, Jann 65, 154, 155, 183, 190, 217
Whalen, Phil 21
White, Joshua 169
White Heaven 17
The Who 153
Whole Earth Catalog 75, 77
"Wild West Festival" 206-7
Wildwood Boys 27
Wilhelm, Mike 44, 45, 114, 117, 179, 217
William Penn & his Pals 56, 57, 59
Willis, Ellen 191
Willner, Phyllis 119
Wilson, Wes 85
Wolfe, Tom 61, 75, 79, 118, 121, 125
Woodstock 206

Yanovsky, Zal 115
Yippies 189
Young, Neil 139
Youngbloods 137

Zappa, Frank 97, 151

A C K N O W L E D G M E N T S

My thanks to John Crosby, Julia Honeywell at Ace, Nic Harcourt at WDST in Woodstock, Alec Palao, David Fricke, Edward Helmore, Charles Perry, Steve Turner, Harvey Kubernik, Tony Peake, Alan Robinson at Edsel/Demon, David Reynolds and Monica Macdonald at Bloomsbury, Anne Yarowsky and Melissa Roberts at Simon & Schuster, Ed Sanders, Greg Shaw, Lou Adler, Carl Gottlieb, John Platt, and David Rubinson.

P I C T U R E S

My thanks to the following individuals and organizations who supplied photographs and illlustrations for inclusion in this book (list in alphabetical order followed by page numbers). Graphic ephemera and objet trouvé from the Simon Jennings Archive, special studio photography by Ben Jennings: 3, 4, 6/7, 8, 20/21, 24, 27, 28, 32, 41, 42/43, 52, 72, 74, 100, 102, 128, 146, 148, 150, 166, 182, 186/187, 204/205. Gene Anthony: 5, 32, 38, 76, 82, 84, 110. Associated Press: 122, 136, 142, 156. Robert Crumb: 162. Herb Greene: 16, 18, 34, 44, 62, 64, 66, 68, 78, 86, 88, 90, 92, 94, 98, 104, 108, 112, 113, 116, 117, 126, 138, 180, 212. Lisa Law: 58, 124, 144. Magnum: Thomas Höpker 136, Dennis Stock 142. Alec Palao: 60, 120, 220. Redferns: 106. Rex Features: 163, 218. The Selvin Collection: 50, 54, 70, 96, 140, 168, 178, 196. Jon Sievert: 80, 82, 170. Jerry Stoll: 10, 12/13, 14, 22, 30, 48, 49. Universal Pictorial Press: 40. United Press International Ltd: 184/185. USIS: 42/43. Baron Wolman: 36, 84, 130, 134/135, 152, 154, 158/159, 159, 160, 164, 172, 176, 188, 192/193, 198, 202, 208/209, 218. Every effort has been made to contact the owners of copyright photographs included in this volume; Bloomsbury Publishing Plc would appreciate any uncredited copyright holders contacting them.

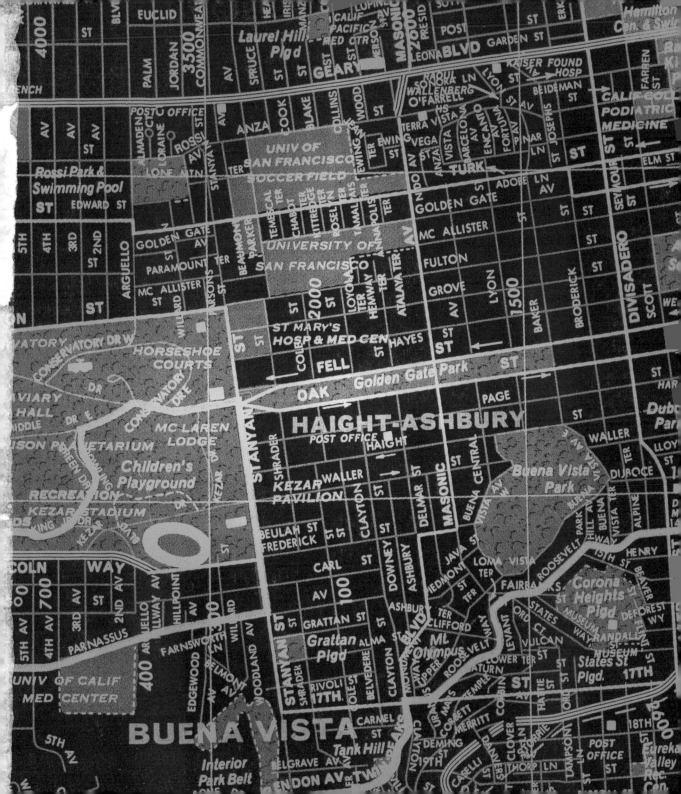

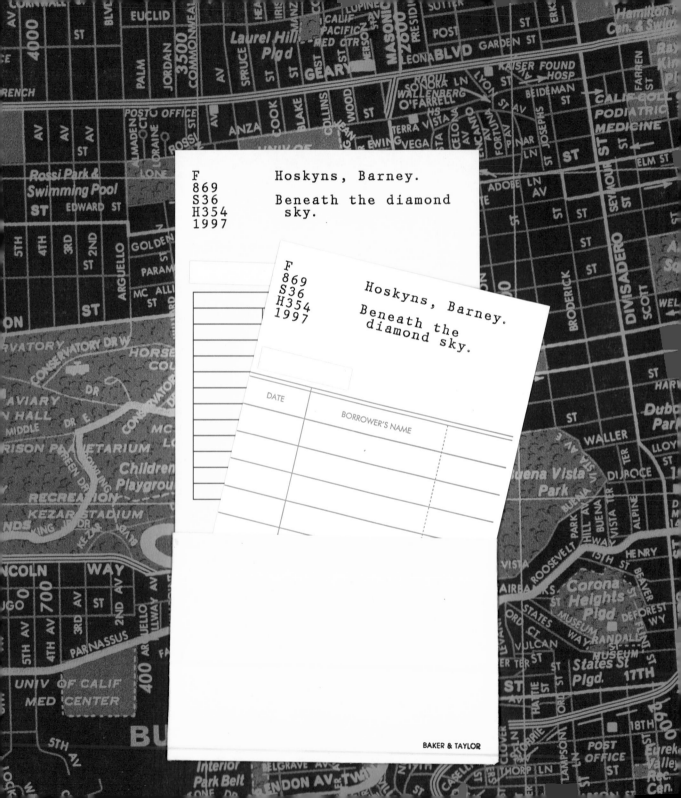